JOURNEY THROUGH THE HOODS
From Poverty to Million Dollar Real Estate Agent

Markus Smith, Ph.D.

Copyright © 2021
Journey Through the Hoods, by Markus Smith, Ph.D.

All rights reserved. No part of this book may be used or reproduced in any manner whatsoever without written permission of the author.

Author has tried to recreate events, locales and conversations from his memories of them. In order to maintain their anonymity in some instances, some of the names of individuals and places, along with some identifying characteristics and details such as physical properties, occupations and places of residence may have been changed.

Although the author and publisher have made every effort to ensure that the information in this book was correct at press time, the author and publisher do not assume and hereby disclaim any liability to any party for any loss, damage, or disruption caused by errors or omissions, whether such errors or omissions result from negligence, accident, or any other cause.

Published by CLC Publishing, LLC.
Mustang, OK 73064

Printed in the United States of America

Edited by Heidi Owens
Book Design by Crystal Manu
Cover Design by Stellar Creative LLC

ISBN: 978-1-7363318-4-2

REVIEWS

"Education can truly change the trajectory of one's life. If in doubt, I highly recommend that you read Markus Smith's life story that he courageously shares in his book, JOURNEY THROUGH THE HOODS. It is a powerful testimony to not only the value of education, but the impact others can have in defying the destiny of demographics. Markus's life choices were impacted by his mother's high expectations, his friends' parents who provided a protective barrier from the streets, and the education professionals that saw a diamond in the rough. However, one cannot deny that Markus's own grit and vision motivated him each step of the way. Markus knows that you must be laborious before you can be glorious. He truly personifies a favorite saying of mine: If It Is To Be, It Is Up To Me."

Mike Turpen, Attorney at Law and Civic Volunteer

"Dr. Smith's book, "Journey Through the Hoods," is a wonderful testament to the better sides of ourselves. Through the tale of his own process of self-discovery, Dr. Smith details the importance of education, family, tolerance, and understanding. These values are desperately needed in today's world, and they are the same values that have made Dr. Smith the success that he is!"

Collin Walke, Legislator and Attorney

"Dr. Smith shows vulnerability and strength as he recounts his journey from being a child 'candy dealer' for school lunch money, to selling million-dollar real estate as a successful agent in Oklahoma. Through stories of resiliency and relationships, Smith's story shows depth in the true emotions that go hand in hand with life's true journey, giving the reader access to a story of perseverance and evolution, which show the full magnitude of a human's capability. A powerful read for us all!"

The Reverend Dr. Shannon Fleck, Nonprofit Director and Pastor

"Inspiration comes in many forms—Dr. Smith reinforces how hard work and determination can overcome insurmountable odds. Journey Through the Hoods proves dreams can and do come true!"

Dr. Steven Bloomberg, President, Southeast Arkansas College

DEDICATION

I would like to thank everyone that has supported me throughout my nearly 50-year journey. There are way too many people to list on this page. You know who you are and this book is dedicated to you.

Love you all,

~ Markus

The road has been bumpy. Life got a rough start. But I was surrounded by my family, I was loved, I was fed, and I was cared for.

But I was also surrounded by poverty, racism, prejudice, gangs, violence, drugs, prostitution, and everything that comes with all of that.

Allow me to paint a picture of my story…

Lights are hung on all the buildings in town and even though the sky is a perfect blue, there's a cool crisp in the air that shocks your lungs with every breath. It's winter in Oklahoma, and Christmas is coming.

It should be a time of joy and excitement. People should be preparing for the holiday, sharing their plans for travel, family visits, feasts, and gifts. But not here. Not in my neighborhood. I never got to feel or hear that joy or excitement that other people talk about. However, what I did hear were the gunshots that were so prevalent in our neighborhood even during the holidays.

Our neighborhood is located in a very poor and very rough part of Northeast Oklahoma City – often referred to as the "east side". Our Christmas wasn't filled with colorful reds, greens, silvers, and golds of other neighborhoods. We didn't have a tree covered in tinsel with presents crammed beneath it.

The most I see of "real" Christmas is the occasional commercial or Christmas show that would play on our 12" broken black and white TV. The only "snow" we saw at Christmas was the fuzzy display on that TV screen as we worked the antenna to bring in a channel as clearly as possible.

Those shows and commercials would sometimes give my young mind some hope. I'd feel a twinge of the Christmas spirit building inside. But it never lasted long. The truth was simple; we were poor, and Christmas never came. Not in the way a child expects it to, anyway.

There was never much talk about these things in my home, and when I asked about it, I was either hushed or the subject was quickly changed. Sometimes, I feel like my questions anger my parents, and I'm not sure why. They do their best to remain patient with me, but I can tell they do not feel the same joy and excitement I am seeing when I watch that broken black and white TV.

Even though I know we are poor, my child's mind cannot understand why we don't have Christmas. Why doesn't Santa come? He's the one responsible for all the gifts, right? It shouldn't matter if Mom and Dad have money.

Yet, every year I send a note to the North Pole with my requests, and every year I'm let down. From talking with friends at school, it's the same for them. I begin to wonder if maybe Santa doesn't like kids who live on the east side either. That's ok, though. I'm sure Mom and Dad will come through this year!

After dinner, as I'm getting ready for bed, I hear Mom and Dad talking quietly. I'm certain they are discussing what they're going to get me for Christmas, so I slowly sneak back down the hallway. Just out of sight, I'm able to hear their low voices. I strain to listen...

I hear them talking about money. It doesn't sound like a happy conversation. Young as I am, I begin to feel confused and sense that I probably shouldn't be listening, yet I can't stop. As I listen, I can tell my mom is starting to cry. Dad sounds serious and sad. As it turns out, they are talking about Christmas – but not in the joyful way I had anticipated.

I hear things like, "But, how long can we go without electricity?" and, "Would it be better to pay the electric bill, and go without heat for a month? It's chilly, but not the coldest winter we've had." "We need them to have something to open Christmas morning; maybe we can skimp on groceries for a couple of months?"

My parents were sitting there, in front of our nearly bare Christmas tree strung with popcorn and a few mismatched ornaments deciding which bills to ignore to make sure my sister and I had a few gifts to open Christmas morning.

This was the moment I first realized our reality – we were poor.

***

As a kid, you don't typically pay attention to things such as the size of your home, if the paint is peeling, or if the weeds are tall. You don't understand taxes, the importance of good quality schools, or whether or not it's normal to hear gunshots at night.

The fact of the matter is, as a kid, you usually just accept your reality as "normal". Especially when all those who live around you are living in the same manner. Everyone's homes look similar, their cars are similar, the family units are similar, etc. So, you don't stop to think that things could be different.

I didn't feel all that different growing up in my neighborhood. It was the early '70s, and we had just moved to Oklahoma. My dad (Black) was an Air Force veteran who met my mom (Japanese) while stationed in Japan. She spoke very little English, yet was determined to do what she could to help my dad do the best for our family.

It may sound as though we were a typical family: Dad, Mom, myself, and my baby sister. However, what made us "different" was the fact that we were a mixed-race family. That may not seem like a big deal to some, but in the early to mid-'70s in Oklahoma, it was still a very big deal.

Although my dad was a veteran and had served his country, he was still seen as "less than" and struggled to find work outside of the military. This meant living in poorer areas where gang activity – and all that comes with it – was prevalent. Mom did what she could to help, but once it was known that she was married to a black man, she also struggled to find work.

People didn't only hate black people, they hated people who *didn't* hate black people. Being married to a black man, my mom would be called some of the ugliest of names. Names like "nigger-lover." As a small child, I may not have understood what this meant at first, but I could vividly hear the snarl in their voices and see them sneer as they said it. It was very clearly meant to be mean and hurtful, that much I did know.

My mom experienced racism from two sides: being married to a black man, as well as being Japanese. People still remembered WWII all too well and were still angry with Japanese people. Let's not forget that it was just 30 years prior, in 1942 during WWII, when 120,000 Japanese-Americans were forced into internment camps because they were deemed a threat to our national security following the attack and bombing at Pearl Harbor. Therefore, racial slurs were spewed at both my parents, and mom, especially, was often told to "go back home" or to "go bomb another country".

What I didn't understand was why these people didn't like my parents and why they would call them names. I knew my dad was a hard worker and I knew my mom wanted to help, yet these people would turn them away for being a "nigger" and a "nigger-lover."

It may not have made much sense to me at the time, but it certainly made me angry. It made me not like those racist people, and sometimes, I even felt afraid of them. The ugliness they projected always made me wonder how mean they could become. I learned at a young age to keep my distance and not trust anyone who behaved in such ways.

My anger only grew as I got older and I believed it was because of those people that we remained in our neighborhood. It was why mom and dad struggled and couldn't provide more for my sister and me. It was why we lived in the 'hood.

You see, when we moved to Oklahoma in 1974, it had only been 7 years before in *Loving v. Virginia* (1967) that laws banning interracial marriage were found to be unconstitutional by the U.S. Supreme Court. And Oklahoma was one of many southern states that had banned interracial marriages. The Civil Rights Act of 1964 had passed about a decade before, and It was just 20 years prior in *Brown v. Board of Education* in 1954 when the U.S. Supreme Court outlawed segregation in public schools.

And it had only been 24 years since the U.S. Supreme Court ruled in 1950 that, in essence, the University of Oklahoma and other institutions of higher education, could no longer refuse to admit Blacks and other people of color into their institutions in the *McLaurin* v. *Oklahoma State Regents* and *Sweatt v. Painter* decisions. It is also important to mention that the Tulsa Race Massacre (also known as the Tulsa Race Riots of 1921) had happened only about 50 years earlier, so it was not yet forgotten. This event, that took place in the predominantly black Greenwood neighborhood in Tulsa ended with hundreds of blacks being killed and all of the thriving black businesses were burned down by an angry white mob, is considered one of the worst incidents of racial violence in U.S. History according to historians and scholars, and it happened right here in Oklahoma.

Racism was still alive and well in the southern parts of the country, and Oklahoma was no exception despite not technically being considered "the South" like states such as Georgia, Alabama, Mississippi, Louisiana. Some Jim Crow laws (segregation between Blacks and Whites) were still in practice but were more embedded within our culture – a sort of *de facto* segregation – as opposed to being required or mandated as was once the case before the Civil Rights Act of 1964.

When we arrived in Oklahoma in the early '70s, people of color still lived in *their* neighborhoods, still went to 'black' schools and we were no exception. There were true black and white schools, and a street, Reno Ave., separated us like the "tracks" you hear of in other stories. We were always told that going south of Reno Ave. was not a good idea if you were black, and the farther south of Reno Ave. you went, the worse it got in terms of racism. I believe it wasn't until around the '80s that Oklahoma City made the move to integrate their schools more, and I was bused across town to the south side of Oklahoma City to attend high school, despite living just blocks away from predominately black schools. Being part of that process is a story of its own, but let me just say, it was not a peaceful, easy transition.

My parents still struggled to obtain even average-paying jobs when we first relocated to Oklahoma, and as a result, we ended up having to live with my great-grandparents for several months in their tiny home in Seminole, Oklahoma. This, of course, affected my parents' ability to provide for us the way they had hoped and intended to. We were poor. I'm not just talking hand-me-down clothes poor, I'm talking government assistance, choose to pay the electric bill or eat kind of poor. And so was everyone else who lived around us.

Living in these conditions, people tend to become desperate and angry. Angry that they are oppressed simply due to the color of their skin. Angry that they are unable to get a decent education and a good-paying job, and therefore unable to afford a decent home and good food, let alone keep the electricity and water on. All of this anger and desperation leads many to a life of crime and violence, and it becomes the only way to have basic needs met. Create a situation where this happens for multiple generations, and you end up with a systemic issue.

One of my uncles got caught in the net of this systemic problem. Unable to find legitimate work, he became a poor product of our environment. He spent almost half of his life in and out of jail and prison starting at the age of 18. In his early 20s he ended up arrested for armed robbery and burglary. Crime was the only way he knew how to meet his basic needs. Granted, I do not condone his actions, but it does paint a picture of how dire one's situation could become in a time when people were denied work and fair wages for simply being black.

We would take family road trips to visit him in prison. My parents, younger sister, and great-grandmother, at times, would all be there to see him. As a young boy, I remember being lifted to be able to talk with him through the small glass window at the prison. Unfortunately, prison didn't "correct" or rehabilitate him. It left him bitter and even angrier with society than before. He never truly recovered after being released from prison in his 40s and ended up drinking himself to death in his late 60s.

It saddens me to think about my uncle and other relatives and friends who ultimately fell victim to the systemic culture – whether directly or indirectly. To think of the lives my uncle and other family members and friends could have lived if given better opportunities. Sure, they had choices and may not have always made the best decisions, but at the end of the day, they were also products of their environment and their choices were few.

Fast forward a few years and you would see that we were still living in the 'hood where it wasn't unusual to see prostitution activity, gang fights and deaths, arrests, drugs, dead bodies lying in a field with gun-shot wounds, and so on. With both of my parents now working, often multiple jobs, I found myself learning how to live the street life. Yes, I had a home and parents who loved me very much, but I quickly became a product of my peripheral environment as well.

Growing up poor and in a violent community can do one of two things to you: it can make you feel jaded and stuck; or it can motivate you to move up and out as soon as possible.

I fell somewhere in between. As I grew older and realized there were better options for my life, I knew I wanted out. I certainly didn't know how, so I remained stuck. I fell into "street life". I found myself drifting more into the streets and hanging out often with close friends; my "homeboys" who were known gang members.

As with most kids who find themselves on this path, some of the gang members became a second family to me. A family you don't easily choose to walk away from once you gain their trust. Even if you know that walking away would be the right thing, even the best thing, there is a part of you that *belongs* there with your homeboys. It becomes what you know and who you are. Just walking away from those you have come to love as family, people you have formed a bond with that cannot be easily broken, isn't something you can just decide to do.

While I'm thankful I eventually found myself drifting away from the gangs, my homeboys, and the violence that surrounded them, in retrospect, I'm also thankful for the hardship that was my younger years. The lessons I learned have remained with me throughout my adult life. While hardened by poverty, gangs, and street life, I was also blessed with compassion and empathy on a level that many will never know or understand.

I may have grown up in the 'hood, but I then moved on to receive my graduation "hood" after earning two Master's degrees and my Ph.D. I now find myself often working in the affluent 'hoods of Oklahoma as a blessed and successful business owner and realtor, well known as the "Suits and Vans Realtor Man".

This is my journey through the various '*Hoods* of life. It's my story and I share it for two reasons: To inspire and motivate you to persevere through whatever adversity you may be facing, and to inspire and motivate you to know there is so much more to the journey. You aren't stuck. You only need to choose to seek a different path. Never let your past determine your future.

-Dr. Markus Smith

PART ONE

LIVING IN THE 'HOOD

CHAPTER ONE

GROWING UP WITH GANGS

When people first meet and get to know me, they're often surprised to learn that I've lived a life immersed with gangs, as gangs were a part of everyday life on the east side. It's not very often that I expose my tattoos, especially my left-arm tattoo sleeve that shows my "East Side" in the typical gang-related Old English lettering and "Never Forget Where You Came From" tattoo in a signature-script-font equipped with a headshot of a gang member wearing a bandana, graffiti, a gang member behind bars, a gang member seated while holding a gun, an angel – you know, all of the things that are typically found in a tattoo[1]. Many people often make quick judgments when they see tattoos, let alone gang-related or inspired tattoos. Being a prominent real estate agent, and professional in my community, I often feel as though I need to hide my tattoos, to hide that part of my past in order to retain the trust and respect of my community.

---

[1] See photos #1 and #2

Of course, after learning more about me and seeing my tattoos, it's often followed with several questions. The first usually being, "What do those mean?"

My observation throughout life has been that if you are not from Oklahoma, your perception of Oklahoma is a land of tornadoes, oil rigs, dirt roads farmers, cowboys, Native Americans, tumbleweeds, horses, cows, and rural country. Seldom do people think about gangs and gang violence when Oklahoma is mentioned. Those things are typically reserved for L.A. and other big cities.

Growing up on the east side of Oklahoma City was rough. It is still a rougher part of the city, but in the 70s and 80s, this was especially true. Gang violence was at an all-time high. As time went on, gang violence began to taper off. By the late 90s, things had simmered quite a bit compared to the previous two decades. However, that didn't mean gang activity ceased altogether.

During the mid-1980s, gang activity and violence significantly increased throughout the state. The Oklahoma State Bureau of Narcotics and Dangerous Drugs Control Intelligence Division released a report[2] in 1991 that estimated as many as 9,000 gang members in the Oklahoma City Metro alone. This was due in part to the arrival and invasion of Los Angeles-based street gang members known as Crips and Bloods. They came to Oklahoma to expand their drug dealing operations that primarily revolved around "crack" cocaine. We referred to it at times as "rocks" – or, as you may hear in some rap songs referred to as "slangin' rocks" which simply meant selling crack. I knew the gang violence on the east side had become well known and recognized when we (Oklahoma) were mentioned in a media sample that appeared in the gangsta rapper Ice Cube's song "Summer Vacation" in 1991:

> "Top of the news tonight, gangs from South Central, Los Angeles which are known for their drive-by shootings have migrated into East St. Louis, leaving three dead and two others injured. No arrests have

---

[2] "Preliminary Analysis of the Crips and Bloods"

been made. Police say this is a nationwide trend, with similar incidents occurring in Texas, Michigan, and *Oklahoma*."

Though gangs in Oklahoma were only starting to receive media attention in the mid-1980's, they had always been a part of the culture and environment that I grew up with. They affected other family mem-bers and friends throughout my life.

Sadly, my cousin Mike, who was like a little brother to me, became a victim of gang violence in our neighborhood. Though he was able to keep himself out of gangs and gang activity, for the most part, he was still a very unfortunate product of our environment and ended up in the wrong place at the wrong time. In 1999, Mike and his friend, Dante, went to pick up another friend, Chris.

The incident occurred when Mike was slowly pulling out of the driveway after picking up Chris, who was now in the backseat. Some guys came out of the house and on to the lawn throwing up gang signs. In response, I believe either Dante or Chris threw up a gang sign back at the guys; commonly referred to as "hit 'em up." From there, one of the guys who was standing in the front yard with his homeboys pulled out a gun and started shooting at the car.

My cousin tried to reverse the car and drive off while dodging bullets. Two shots hit him; one in the head and one in the chest. He still tried to drive away. He died three or four blocks from the scene. Local law enforcement and the media concluded that the event was "gang-related." My cousin was only 24 years old.

I will never forget the anger I felt, the vengeance and retaliation that was brewing within me. I remember being at the funeral services and several family members came rushing up to me and my best friend Moe. They begged us not to retaliate against those that had taken our cousin away from us. It was definitely a family intervention taking place at the burial site, as several family members knew what Moe and I were ca-pable of, especially during that time in our lives.

I was 28 and Moe was 29. Some of you may be asking what I was going to do as a 28-year-old in retaliation for the murder of our cousin.

In an ideal world, many men my age have graduated college, had a career that paid well, a family, nice home, car, etc. But for me, even at 28, my life was still in the streets hanging with my homeboys doing dumb stuff. My life at that time was still pretty chaotic, but I hid it well from those closest to me. I will just say that it was for the best that local law enforcement found the person responsible for our cousin's murder before we did.

Another one of my uncles also became a victim of gang violence. It was another circumstance of being in the wrong place at the wrong time according to several family members. According to my father, in 1999, my uncle, his girlfriend, and a mutual friend decided to go to a convenience store late one evening on the east side to pick up some snacks. My uncle went inside while the others remained in the car. While inside the store, he got into an altercation with another customer. The altercation escalated to a point at which the cashier threatened to call the police. The customer immediately exited the store while my uncle continued to purchase his items. As soon as my uncle exited the store, the other customer was standing outside and pulled out a gun. He shot my uncle in the neck, severing his carotid artery. My uncle fell to the ground where he bled to death. He was only 34 years old. Sadly, there was never much investigation into the murder of my uncle, who was like a big brother to me. Because he was black, in a black neighborhood notorious for gang activity, it was chalked up to being gang-related and that was pretty much that.

Gangs and gang-activity over the years affected several others who were close to me. One of my homeboys got caught up in the gang life, became a drug dealer, and ended up shooting and killing someone during a drug deal gone wrong. He was sentenced to life without parole at the age of 18 years old. He is 46 years old and still in prison.

One of my other homeboys who was cruising one of the popular strips on Northeast 23rd St. one Friday evening was shot in the head. He died in the parking lot of a popular fast food chain while still in his car. One of my dear friends, who had absolutely nothing to do with gangs, was shot point blank in the face while in his customized car because he refused to get out and allow the gunman to steal it. Car-jacking was prevalent, especially during the late 80s and 90s on the east side. If you had a customized car or truck during this time, you were most likely packing a gun (and I was) and doing your best not to catch a red light, as that was typically when car-jackings occurred. It was easier for the "jacker" to "jack" your ride if you were at a red light or a stop. There's a scene in the 1993 movie "Menace II Society" that exemplifies this well.

Unfortunately, I could go on and on discussing the countless friends and family I have lost due to the gang violence that plagued my community.

The crime and violence increased to the point where gangs took over the area. Gang members would feed off the fear and use it to recruit others into their way of life with promises of money, protection, and a sense of belonging. Unfortunately, as the gang activity rose, so did the crime that comes with it. Drugs, prostitution, gang violence, and drive-by shootings became regular and normal activities.

I remember the sound of gunshots being a normal neighborhood sound, like the sirens of a firetruck or a train passing. If we were outside playing and they sounded close enough, we'd hit the ground in an attempt to avoid being shot by a stray bullet. The terror of hitting the ground and seeing the sparks from the bullets grazing the concrete a few feet away from your face would make most people piss their pants. But not us, as we were used to this, even as kids. This was our normal.

Once we knew the coast was clear, we were back up and doing whatever we had been doing. Even during my adolescent and young adult years, I cannot recall how many times that my homeboys and I had to dive on the concrete or behind a car, duck across the front seat of a car, or even run into an abandoned building or house to avoid being shot.

The violence became so prevalent that it was nearly impossible to live in our area and not be exposed to and affected by the gang activity.

Whether a family member or you became part of a gang, or your family was harmed by gang activity, it touched us all.

People are not born thinking they want to become part of a gang. In fact, most people don't even realize it's happening until one day they wake up and the realization just hits: "I'm in a circle of gang members."

When I talk about gangs, I'm not talking about your average school clique that people refer to as their "gang". I'm talking about street-hardened criminal gangs. That's where I found myself; associated with some of the most violent gang members and drug dealers primarily in Oklahoma City, as well as some from other states (California and Texas) who had relocated to Oklahoma, who I would later see end up incarcerated or dead.

You see, when we first moved to Oklahoma back in the early '70s, it was extremely challenging for my mother, me, and my sister. Let me go back a few years to better explain. My mother and father met while my father was serving in the Air Force and stationed in Tokyo, Japan. They actually met at the Yokota Air Base in 1969. He was 21 and my mother was 22[3].

A year later they were married in 1970 and the following year in 1971 I was born. About a year after I was born, we moved to Cheyenne, Wyoming and lived on the Francis E. Warren Air Force Base. My mother's Japanese parents were extremely upset and fearful of us moving to the U.S. and opposed the relocation. Their fear stemmed from how they saw blacks treated in the U.S.

They saw the media coverage of blacks being beaten, lynched, hosed down with fire hoses, and so much more. So, my Japanese grandparents[4] were extremely fearful of how the three of us would be treated in the U.S. with my dad being black, my mom being Japanese, and me being biracial. My Japanese grandfather, especially, as he was still trying to cope with me leaving Japan when I was just a baby. He loved me so much, as I was his first grandchild, and he and I really bonded that

---

[3] See photo #3
[4] See photo #4

year before we left for Wyoming[5]. It's no wonder why I was named after him: Markus "Shintaro" Smith.

In 1973, while still residing in Wyoming, my sister was born. The following year, my father was deployed to Turkey and an extremely difficult decision had to be made – my mother, who barely spoke any English and now with me (2 years-old) and my sister who was still a baby – decided to move to Seminole, Oklahoma to live with my great-grandparents. We were not allowed to travel and live with my father because he was going to be stationed on a missile base.

Of course, this upset my Japanese grandparents even more and they were even more fearful, as we would be moving to the south – the "country" south at that, as Seminole, Oklahoma, even to this day is still a fairly rural city with a population of about only 7200 people. But for my Japanese grandparents, they knew and witnessed the treatment of blacks was far worse in the "south" and they were extremely concerned.

But despite the pleas from my Japanese grandparents for us to move back to Japan to live with them, my mother made the very difficult decision to move to Seminole to live with my father's grandparents. What made the decision so difficult, was that moving back to Japan would have been safer. It would have provided more comfort, my mom spoke the language, and we would have had all that we needed. A stark contrast to moving to rural Oklahoma.

My mother moving to Seminole was like being dropped off in a foreign country with no money, not knowing anyone, and not being able to communicate with anyone because you did not speak the language. And you have 2 small children! I cannot even imagine doing that myself now, and especially if I was a young adult.

Despite all of this, the decision was made. The main reason being because she wanted to establish a better relationship with my father's side of the family, as she really did not know any of them. She also felt, quite simply, that this is what a wife should do for her husband. She wanted to continue to be immersed in the cultures, norms, and language

---

[5] See photo #5

of the U.S. as she believed that would be extremely important for me and my sister. Truly a sacrifice.

In 1974, my mother, me, and my sister found ourselves living with my great-grandparents ("Ginny" and "Allen") in Seminole, who were extremely poor. I couldn't say "Granny" correctly when I was little, so I called her "Ginny" my entire life.

And it must have been during the summer, because I recall being extremely hot during the evenings and having a bowl of water near the bed. My mom would often take this small hand towel and wipe us down in hopes that what little draft of air would come in through the window near our bed would provide some cool comfort as the air would hit our bodies that had been moistened by the wet towel. Sadly, this method would be used throughout my young life, as I do not recall us having a home with a decent air conditioner until I was in high school.

Over the course of a few months, this decision to move to Seminole had proven to be a terrible mistake by my mother. I am not really sure if it was simply due to the language-barrier, the different customs, or the age of my great-grandparents (who were in their 60s at the time), but my mother felt extremely isolated and alone and lacking the basic necessities for us[6].

And to make matters worse, we barely had enough to eat, as my great-grandparents were poor. My father sent money when he could but it was not very much, and the money he did send to my mother, she would split it with Ginny and Allen to help them out as well.

There was really no communication between her and my great-grandparents. This resulted in my mother having a nervous breakdown and having to be taken to the hospital by my grandmother (my dad's mother) who drove down from Oklahoma City. My mother remained in the hospital for a few days. When my father found out, he strongly encouraged my mother to move us back to Japan with her parents while he was in Turkey.

---

[6] See photo #6

However, in an attempt to be this "good wife" and doing everything she could for her husband, she told herself she would simply "tough it out" and remain in Seminole. Of course, my mother's mindset at that time stemmed from her very traditional Japanese culture upbringing in which a wife was to be extremely submissive and loyal to her husband and his family and to do everything in her power to make them happy.

Nevertheless, after a few more weeks things still had not gotten any better for us. Therefore, my father requested to be transferred back to the U.S. When his request was denied, he requested and was granted an honorable discharge from the Air Force and that was the end of his short 7-year military career. He chose family over career.

A few months later, and now reunited with my father, we found ourselves relocated to Oklahoma City and residing in one of the poorest and crime-ridden neighborhoods on the east side of the city. The Carverdale neighborhood was a rough neighborhood back in 1974 and sadly continues to be one of the poorest neighborhoods even today.

During this time, it was extremely difficult for both of my parents to find good work based on their circumstances; not having a college degree, no professional experience, and being an interracial couple. Money was extremely tight, as my father had lost his military income.

Here was this woman who came to this foreign country, married to an American veteran, looking to better her life and raise her family. She faced discrimination and racism. Was she bitter? Did this upset her? Absolutely, but more importantly, it disappointed her, as she believed the things she and her parents viewed on television could not be as bad as the media was portraying it to be in terms of the treatment of blacks. But her anger and disappointment fueled her with this drive to be the best – to show the racists that she would make it here in America on her own terms, even if they did not want her here.

She pressed on and worked harder than I've ever seen someone work. She never quit, she always made sure we were taken care of and I knew we were loved. I will always admire her for her determination and tenacity.

My mom understood that racist attitudes were not something that people are born with. Racism is something that is taught; a learned behavior. The best way to combat racism is with the power of education. Therefore, she believed that the "mean" people were simply lacking this education and it was for me to educate them and open up their hearts to see me as a person and a human being and not judge me for the color of my skin. According to her, mean people acted the way they did because they were afraid of the man that I would become.

During those years in Oklahoma, where some Jim Crow laws were still being practiced, there was no way either of my parents were going to find work that paid well. My father would eventually obtain a job at a food-packing plant.

Unfortunately, my dad injured his back while on the job that resulted in several major surgeries. He wasn't able to return to any type of work for years, which resulted in a lot of financial pressure falling on my mother. She still hadn't learned to speak much English, so the language barrier, compounded with the racial issues, made it extremely difficult for her to find work.

But she never gave up. She would search, and search, and search some more. She would take on any job that she could. This eventually led to her having various jobs at any given time. One of the jobs she held included cleaning old, dirty, filthy, run-down hotel rooms. There were times, as a child, I would go to work with my mom. I vividly remember just how dirty the rooms were. The smell and filth are things you don't easily forget. I even recall her working a second job at a McDonald's. In retrospect, I know I gained my work ethic observing my mom struggle and work extremely hard.

But she had also instilled within me the importance of an education, as her hope was that I would never have to work under the same poor working and societal, racist conditions she had to endure.

I can remember as a young child my mom coming home at night, tired and sore. She would sit me down at our broke down kitchen table in our little old house and work to teach me math. She had hopes and dreams that someday I would be an engineer. Barely able to keep her own eyes open, she would explain to me the doors education would open. She taught me that despite the color of my skin and the obstacles that I would endure, education would help to reduce the racist and prejudiced attitudes I may face. She understood that education would enable me to surround myself with other educated people who would either have grown out of any prejudices they learned early on, or have the maturity to look past them.

We worked on math well beyond my grade level. It was hard, and while I certainly didn't enjoy the extra work, struggling to believe it would ever really help me, it was the look in her eyes that made me a willing participant. It was pure joy for me to see her face light up with happiness when I would get a math problem right. That happiness, I believe, is what fueled her soul with the energy to continue those tutoring lessons late into the evening despite being completely exhausted.

Despite these moments with my mother that often took me to a happy place in my mind, the reality would slap me in the face the following morning as I put on my floodin' jeans, Velcro-strapped Payless shoes, and stained t-shirt that served as a sad reminder that we were poor. Times were tough growing up.

There was a time when things got so rough that we had to move in with my cousins. I think I was 10 or 11. That made it a total of 10 of us in a 1200 square foot home that had 2 bedrooms, only 1 full bathroom, and another add-on type room that was poorly constructed but served as a sleeping area for us boys. The house was not in the best condition, missing trim around doors, no carpet in some rooms, torn up laminate flooring, not insulated well, and didn't have the best AC or heater[7]. Summers were scorching and winters were freezing. I vividly recall having to share a twin bunk bed with 2 of my cousins, while my other 2 cousins got to share a bunk bed. My baby sister had a bed to herself since she was the only girl among the 6 of us kids. I also remember how the 5 of us boys would play a game of basketball to determine

---

[7] See photo #7

the winner who would have to only sleep with one other boy in the bunk bed. It was miserable sleeping in a twin bunk bed with 2 other boys. They were my "brothers," but it was miserable and uncomfortable nonetheless.

I also recall all of the boys having to shower together to conserve hot water for my parents, my cousins' parents, and my sister. The five of us boys crammed into the shower like sardines made us master the quick, in and out shower. We may not have been squeaky clean, but we were clean, healthy, and loved, and that was what was most important. I did not realize that at the time, but I have often looked back to those days and appreciated what my aunt and uncle sacrificed to take us all in. That is what family does.

I *know* it was especially hard on my mom living with my cousins. She was extremely stressed out. Whether that was from the embarrassment of having to move in with them or the fact that we remained in the same position; poor, in need of help, and living in a violent community. I remember her having what could only be described as another nervous breakdown. Seeing my mom sobbing nearly every day broke my heart and I tear up every time I think about this. I wished there was something I could do to help her and us. To see how hard she had worked and to find us in this position planted a seed within me to want to better my life so that I could always take care of her. She did not deserve this. Nevertheless, here we were.

Once dad was able to get back to work, my sister and I became latchkey kids. We were left alone after school to fend for ourselves and each other. There was no one home to supervise us. Mom and dad couldn't afford milk and cheese from the grocery store, let alone any kind of babysitter. Back in the 70s and early 80s, there weren't electronics to keep kids occupied and in the house. Even if there had been, we certainly wouldn't have been able to afford them.

So, my sister and I did what all kids in our neighborhood did; we ran the streets. We had our friends and other "moms" on our block. Our friends' moms would do their best to look out for all of us kids and keep us in line whenever they could. You've heard the phrase "It takes a village"? That was certainly the case in our neighborhood. We all became like one big family, looking out for each other, protecting each other, and keeping everyone in line.

As kids, we saw the drugs and violence going on, but we were much more concerned with having fun. Everything happening around us was just part of the scenery. Seeing a dead body on the ground became a normal sight. Having to hit the ground ourselves during a drive-by shooting was a normal Friday. Seeing a prostitute who had been beaten by her pimp was normal. Seeing drug deals just a few feet away from my house was a daily occurrence, as we lived in a home for several years next door to a run-down apartment complex that provided the arena for drug deals and prostitutes having sex in the parking lots.

We thought some of the "OGs" (or original gangsters, who were old gang members) were being pretty cool when they would give us money for candy if we ran a package down to the corner for them or came running back to let them know if we saw any "po-po's" (police) in the neighborhood. We didn't know at the time as kids that we were helping in gang and drug activities. We just thought the "cool guys" liked us, and that made *us* cool.

Who would have thought some kids just out having a good time would be a target of drug dealers and gang members looking to grow the gang? But that was life in the 'hood. Start them young, grow them hard, put them to work. Being poor and unsupervised made us easy targets. A few bucks to buy the treats our parents couldn't afford was the ticket to our loyalty.

It's how most of the kids ended up street-hardened and on the fast-track to prison life or the grave.

These were normal occurrences around the 'hood. As far as we knew, this was how it was everywhere. We didn't know it could be different.

CHAPTER TWO

HAND-ME-DOWNS AND 'GUVMENT' CHEESE

By the time I entered my 5th Year Center and middle school years, I had a deeper realization that we were poor. I lacked the name brand clothes and shoes that I had saw others wearing. Rather than Nike shoes and Levi's, my sister and I wore hand-me-down clothes and shoes. If our shoes were new, they came from Goodwill or Payless Shoes. Wearing Pro Wings, also known as the poor man's, wanna-be Nike shoes, were the worst, as the kids at school were relentless in making fun of me. Our clothes were cheap all the way around.

It had always been this way, but as young kids, no one pays attention to these details. Heading into middle school, it seemed *everyone* paid attention. There was no hiding the fact that my family lived in poverty. Funny thing is, no one in our school was rich. There were just different levels of poor.

To this day, when I tell someone familiar with Oklahoma City that I lived in the Carverdale neighborhood in the early 70s and 80s, and went to Moon Middle School, their reaction is always, "Damn! You was HOOD!" You see, our school was located right in the middle of the east side, the most impoverished black area of the city.

As if the clothes and shoes weren't enough, there was further proof of our financial status in the school lunch line. We 'qualified' for free lunch at school. Back then, there were two lines for school lunch: the Free Lunch line, and the Paid Lunch line. All kids were not given the same food.

In my mind, it was the 'Poor' line and the 'Rich' line. Kids in the poor line received food like fried meat products that at least looked like chicken fingers, some type of mashed up 'something', and if we were lucky, a piece of old fruit. In contrast, the rich kids received things like hamburgers, nachos, and French fries. I was thankful to have some rich friends at school, as they would often give their leftover lunch food portions to me, as they could see that my free lunch portion of food was not enough to fill me up, especially since we had light dinners and no breakfast at home. The nachos were always my favorite!

I know this sounds crazy, but when I ate the leftover nachos from my friends, the cheese tasted *different*. It was a good kind of different, like how I imagined cheese was supposed to taste. I was used to the "government cheese", or "guvment" cheese as we called it, as that was what those of us who grew up on food stamps and assistance ate. It was all our parents could afford. On the other hand, I'm sure some of you reading this right now are smiling or laughing as you may still say "guvment", or at least still hear it as you read. Urban Dictionary has even added "guvment" to their list of accepted words.

I was so used to seeing cheese come as a block in a long rectangular, white cardboard box, much like how Velveeta cheese comes packaged today. I never knew that the "good" cheese came individually wrapped, or in a liquid form for nachos until I reached middle school and ate the leftovers from friends. I thought all cheese came in a long block and had to be sliced with a dull butter knife. We never had consistent slices, either. There would be slices that were perfectly sliced for a sandwich and then there were slices that were thick enough for 5 sandwiches. But I did not dare complain! In fact, I was sure to thank Mom for putting that thick slice on my sandwich. It was thick and chewy, but I ate it. I just ate that guvment cheese sandwich with the biggest smile on my face, thankful to have something to eat.

After getting a taste of the rich food at school and knowing my parents didn't have the money for me to be able to eat from the rich food line, I became compelled to start hustlin' and slangin' candy at school. This provided me with the additional money to be able to buy nachos or a cheeseburger for myself. It felt good having my own, rather than taking leftovers from my friends.

To be sure we never ran out of money for the tastier middle school lunch, my cousins and I would arrive at school early and walk down to the nearest convenience or grocery stores before class began. We would stuff candy in our inside jacket pockets when no one was looking. Those pockets were torn at the bottom, allowing the candy to fill up our jackets. We would then sell the stolen candy to our friends once we got to school. Straight profit! It was the beginning of my hustlin' and dealing days. The candy dealer was born.

As a young boy, it started becoming clear even outside of school, that we had less than some of my friends. I had a desire to look like them and fit in. I wanted to be seen as cool, and I knew that wasn't going to happen by wearing ill-fitted hand-me-down clothes. It wasn't the best option, but I figured out a way to get the clothes I needed.

I loved spending the night with one of my best friends in middle school. Although his parents were not rich by any means, as they lived in a pretty rough and impoverished area on the south side of OKC, they still had more than us. I especially loved spending the weekend there, as I would intentionally pack some of my friend's good, name brand clothes to take back home with me. Of course, I would always say it was a mistake, but it was very intentional. My friend must have understood because he was never angry with me when my mom would catch them in the laundry and make me return them. I'm sure he knew. I mean, who accidentally takes someone's Levi's jeans home every time they visit? I'm not sure if he felt bad for me or just didn't want to embarrass me further by bringing it up. Either way, he was a good friend. I probably could've just asked to borrow them, and he would've said yes, but I was always too embarrassed.

His Levi's were the first *good* pair of jeans I ever wore. The problem, however, was that my friend was smaller than I was. My workaround for this was to sometimes go days without eating so I could lose weight to fit into his jeans. I recall one time that I dropped so much weight in a few days that my mom had to take me to the emergency room. I had simply lost so much weight, so quickly, and I was extremely dehydrated.

Until now, I had never admitted to my mom or anyone else how and why I lost all that weight or became that dehydrated. I put my body through all of that because it was worth it to me. I was so tired of other kids picking on me for the hand-me-down clothes that I had worn for quite some time. The kids were relentless in their teasing, especially if you wore pants or jeans that were too short, or what we called floodin'. These short pants or jeans typically meant that you were wearing hand-me-downs or you had been wearing the same pants and jeans for years because your parents could not afford to buy you new ones as you got taller.

Basically, short jeans that were all around too small, and not of any specific brand, were a badge of poverty. And at that age, kids looked for any reason they could to pick on another kid. My clothes made it easy. Feeling sick and treating my body poorly seemed a small price to pay if it meant the kids would accept me and I could feel cool on the outside.

The irony now is that floodin' has been a fashion statement in some subcultures over the past few years. As an adult, I purposely wear slacks that are too short to either show off my crazy socks or my ankle tattoos when I am rockin' my Vans shoes with my suits and ties. Things I never believed in my wildest dreams as a child that I would ever be able to afford, especially when I think back on those days when wearing hand-me-downs or starving myself to wear my friend's Levi's. No one laughs at my floodin' pants now!

CHAPTER THREE

IT TAKES A VILLAGE

The picture I paint of living on the east side 'hood of Oklahoma City is violent, poor, and bleak. Gangs, death, drugs, prostitution, and everything that comes with it all. While all of that was my reality growing up, it isn't the whole picture. Among the criminal activity and violence, there was also community, love, and protection.

During the days, my sister and I were pretty much on our own. These were the times when the community became family and when the other mothers in the 'hood became our 'hood moms also.

"Mama Moe" was one such significant mom. Her son, Moe, and I became best friends at age 6 and remain so to this day. We lived just a few houses down from each other and would have sleepovers, share dinners, and as we got older, we would run the neighborhoods and streets together.

Mama Moe was a strict disciplinarian though, and if I was going to be in her home, hanging with her son, then she was going to treat me just as she would him. And my parents allowed it. If Moe got in trouble and got a whoopin', so did I. She had zero qualms about letting us have it if we deserved it. And most times, we certainly deserved it.

As we got older, she eased up on the discipline, yet not on her demands for respect for both herself and her home, as well as others. Knowing this, when it came to parties and such, we knew we had to find other venues. We had begun partying at an early age in a way that involved drinking and girls. Moe and I hit this early stage of drinking and partying as soon as we entered high school. But Mama Moe was never going to allow those activities in her home.

Other 'hood moms included Ms. D and Ms. M. Ms. D was very much like Mama Moe when it came to discipline and her demand for respect. We always emphasized "Miss D" to show our respect. She never demanded that we do this, but Moe and I would always see her kids refer to her as "ma'am" so we thought it best and safest to always make sure we said "Ms." when addressing her. She was a hard-working, single mother. Her one son, in particular, Dee, became closer to me than a brother and remains so to this day.

Ms. M was raising four boys of her own, so having me around was easily like having a fifth son in the house. Ms. M demanded respect as well and she was not shy at all in reminding us of this respect by stating over the years: "You will respect me or else!" You never crossed her or disrespected her or she would definitely let you have it. Despite having a small build, she had the strength of Hercules when her palm struck your behind.

Ms. D lived a few miles away and Ms. M lived on my street, so their sons and I all grew up together. While I may not have appreciated the extra discipline then, I can look back now and am so grateful for it. Having these three women in my life, along with my actual mom, did more for me than I will ever know or be able to express.

There were times we would make new friends. Of course, they would show up at one of the 'hood mom's houses with us. Thinking nothing of it, we'd just walk on in per usual. Oh no! That was not going to fly! We weren't to just bring someone into one of their homes. Not without a solid interrogation. And if the barrage of questions did result in satisfactory answers, we would still be counseled on why that kid was not the best option as a friend and would not be allowed into their home. Of course, if all went well, then our new friend would be accepted and loved, just as we were.

During the summers, with my sister and I being out of school, my parents needed more help. Expecting the community to keep watch over us all day, every day was too much to ask or expect. So, we would often spend the summers back in Seminole, Oklahoma with our great-grandparents.

A lot of kids would be thrilled to spend a summer with their great-grandparents. It would be a break from the drudgery of home. But not for us! I may credit my mom with my work ethic, but Ginny certainly had her influence on me as well.

She'd have us up at the crack of dawn to get out into the fields picking wild onions out of the rock-hard Oklahoma clay and pulling pecans from the trees. The Oklahoma sun was blistering and the heat suffocating, even under the shade of those pecan trees. The onion fields were downright unbearable. I recall these summer vacations went on from the ages of 7 through 12. And I say "vacations" with a smirk, as these were no vacations in any sense of the word.

But, she would have us out there working *all* day long. I hated it! The heat. The work. Everything about it. As if life in the 'hood wasn't hard enough, summers in the fields may have been even harder. But looking back at it all, it was rare for a grandson to be able to spend years and time with his great-grandmother. I would pick enough pecans and wild onions in the blistering heat to fill up a stadium today to have my Ginny back.

All of my 'hood moms, and Ginny, were strict disciplinarians. Not because they were just mean moms, but rather because they were busy raising black sons in the ghettos and 'hoods of the east side of Oklahoma City. It was a very stressful job back then with all the violence, gangs, and drugs that were now rampant in our hoods. Many black males ended up incarcerated or dead. The 'hood moms I've mentioned here, along with many others who influenced and protected me along the way, made sure I didn't become one of the statistics.

The more I look back on my past, especially my early upbringing, the more I see the power in the African proverb: "It takes a village to raise a child." There were several other families, friends, and neighbors who cared for not only me and my sister but the other children in our "village" as well.

The 'hood moms and the "village" didn't only raise us kids, they also helped my parents navigate the difficult years. Having this community around us helped to make all of my parents' sacrifices worth it in the end.

While many people today may not view my upbringing as ideal, I'm thankful for it. The experiences I had, the people who affected my life (both positively and negatively) had a great impact on the man I am today. It has led me to use my current situation in life to give back to the people and various low-income and impoverished communities throughout Oklahoma City who gave so much to me.

I am a philanthropist and remain heavily involved within my community, even years before getting into real estate. Even going back to the early 90s during my car club days when I was the president of Low Sensations and Reflections Car Club, I had organized several food and toy drives for the community. I had also volunteered the car club as a spokesperson for the Drug Abuse Resistance Education (D.A.R.E.) Program and spoke to elementary school kids about the dangers of drugs.

Those events followed me throughout the years and when I became a full-time professor back in 2006, I took on the responsibility and organized several charitable events throughout the years that included providing a pallet of copy paper to a local high school in need (apparently copy/printer paper was a scarce commodity back then. I believe teachers in the inner-city public school system can relate); adopting several families every Christmas and providing toys for their children and a nice dinner; campaigning a food drive and donating canned foods to the local food bank; donating school supplies to foundations for Oklahoma City Public Schools; and so much more.

I also served as a mentor and role model to many at-risk kids and adults, those who were more susceptible to joining gangs, doing drugs, and being incarcerated. I would often go back to my 'hood to see family and friends, which I continue to do to this day. They would ask me to "go speak to Mr. Johnson's kid. He's been getting into a lot of trouble." Or they would ask me to "go and see Mrs. Thompson's son, as he's been running around with those gang members again."

I would also become a mentor and speaker to several programs at Oklahoma City Community College (OCCC) that included the Career Transitions Program that was designed to assist those facing financial challenges in obtaining a certificate or degree that would help them obtain employment and financial stability. Many of the individuals in this program were former drug addicts, ex-convicts, had been previously homeless, and those that had simply lived rough lives. And I was honored to be asked to be their mentor and share my journey with them to inspire and motivate them.

I became a mentor for the Students Connecting with Mentors for Success (SCMS) program at OCCC. This program, at the time, focused primarily on black males, as data had shown that black males were the group that had the lowest success rates, grade point averages, test scores, etc. on college campuses throughout the U.S. So, this program assigns mentors with students to help in facilitating academic achievement and the likelihood of graduating.

I loved being able to serve as a mentor to my community and never turned down an opportunity to speak whether it was at another elementary school for my very dear friend Mrs. Heather Meldrum (named Oklahoma City Public Schools Teacher of the Year 2013-2014), who asked that I come and talk to the kiddos about government and the importance of voting; or speaking to the Student Council at U.S. Grant

High School and sharing my journey. I loved it! I am all about giving if you haven't figured it out by now.

However, when I got into real estate and was making significantly more income, I was able to do more with my philanthropic work. My philosophy has always been: The more I make, the more I give. And I gave! Some of the charitable events and sponsorships included: providing backpacks and school supplies for hundreds of elementary school children; purchasing a Christmas tree and decorations for a local nursing home; sponsoring several former students in their fundraisers for sports; sponsoring a local all-women's, professional football team; adopting even more families and their children for Christmas; sponsoring several local high schools and their fundraisers; donating 16,000 meals to a food pantry at a local community college; creating a $25,000 Endowed Scholarship at the University of Central Oklahoma; and so much more.

CHAPTER FOUR

BUSSED TO THE SOUTH SIDE

It was May 1985 and I had just completed my 8th grade year. I was headed for high school! By this time, my circle of friends had expanded beyond just our street. I had friends who lived several streets, or even a couple of neighborhoods away, and we were all looking forward to going into high school together.

Imagine my disdain when I learned I would be one of the kids taking part in the school integration plan. I was going to be bussed to a south side school! I was very angry. At the time, it didn't make any sense to me why some of us were being chosen to leave our comfort zones, our friends, and made to go to school not only with people we didn't know but with *white* people we didn't know. I was afraid of these people! It was very difficult to understand and accept, especially as a 13-year-old.

Please don't get me wrong, there were whites who attended my middle school, but we never had any issues with them because I feel they were in our 'hood and were not going to cause any problems. But the thought of me going to their south side 'hood, so to speak, made me angry.

While those making the school integration decisions understood and felt they were doing me a service, as a kid I felt like I was being punished. Punished for something I could not control. I couldn't control living in a poor part of the city. I couldn't control having dark skin. I couldn't control any of it. So, why was I being forced to leave my 'hood, my home?

Going to a new school is always scary and uncomfortable. At that time, going to a *white* school was even scarier. Adults and the media painted a picture of pure hatred and racism. I was certain that going to this new school was going to be my demise. I anticipated fights, attacks, teachers who wouldn't teach me, kids who would reject me. This was not something I wanted to endure. Of course, these thoughts were coming from a 13-year-old kid, who was very sheltered. All I knew at this age was what I had personally experienced and been taught; that there were white people who hated me for being biracial, and they hated my parents for being in an interracial marriage.

These horrific experiences are what caused many black families to remain on the east side despite the gangs, drugs, and prostitution. It seemed the lesser of two evils. On one hand, you had the violence of the poorer east side, but on the other, you were subject to the violence of racism. It became a situation of feeling safer staying around those who looked like you and who were just as poor as you.

Somehow, being killed by a stray bullet felt less likely than being killed by a racist. So though some may believe I may have been overreacting to my bussing situation, I was angry, but also scared.

My experiences with many white people in my life had been extremely negative up to this point. Now, I was being thrust right into the middle of it – and seemingly alone, as many of my friends were able to remain in school on the east side, which was where black kids predominantly went to school.

A few months before school started, I had to go up to my new school, Southeast High School (SEHS), to enroll in classes for my first semester. I was absolutely angry, apprehensive, and embarrassed. I was angry for having to attend this school on the south side.

I was also angry with my friends in the 'hood who were making fun of me and calling me a "sell-out" for attending SEHS while they would be attending one of the predominantly Black high schools on the east side like Douglass, Northeast, or Milwood.

Nevertheless, I was apprehensive as I did not know how other students and teachers would react to me as being biracial. And I was extremely embarrassed as the only vehicle we had was this old, beat up, and rusted white Monte Carlo that had a horn that would randomly go off and you had to pop the hood to unplug the battery.

I recall my mother telling me stories of times she would be driving it and the horn would just randomly go off as she was driving down the street. And because she did not know how to disconnect the battery, she would just hit the steering wheel multiple times in hopes that it would stop, but it never did.

My biggest fear was pulling up to the school on enrollment day and having this evil and possessed horn go off. Thank goodness the horn was working that morning, but it was still embarrassing to pull up and have several students and teachers see that car and the level of poor that was our life. Some of the students were pointing and laughing while some of them quickly walked away as we approached our parking spot due to the exhaust that made this loud knocking sound as if it were going to explode. I hated this! Such a great first impression.

When I first started school, it was a surreal feeling. I had to cross Reno Ave. This was like going to the other side of the tracks. You weren't supposed to cross Reno. It was basically the dividing line between black and white. Yet here I was, being taken across the line against my will, and thrown to the wolves. I didn't like it at all.

Braced for what I expected to be the worst year of my life, I walked into school. Sure, I got some uncertain glances thrown in my direction.

But, it wasn't as bad as I had expected. Not at school anyway. As it turned out, there was a lot of diversity at the school; Whites, Hispanics, Blacks, and various socio-economic classes.

Some of the kids at Southeast High School were just as poor as we were – they simply lived on the south side. A lot of them lived in trailer homes, apartments, or really small houses; just like us. Their parents worked multiple jobs; just like us. I quickly learned that many of the Hispanic students grew up rough, surrounded by gang violence, drugs, alcohol, and prostitution; just like us. Of course, I didn't know this right away, but as we all became more comfortable with each other, we began opening up and stories were shared. I even started making friends.

I remember thinking I was really going to get picked on or harassed for my hair. My parents had me grow it out. Probably because they couldn't afford for me to get regular haircuts. In any case, it had been long for most of my life. As a little kid, I had been teased and bullied quite a bit, being told I looked like a girl. People would tell me how "pretty" I was. Some even thought I was a girl until they learned otherwise[8]. I just knew these high school kids were going to use my hair as a reason to attack.

Turns out, in the mid-80s, my hair was something to envy! It was the age of Michael Jackson and breakdancing. My hair was no longer something to be embarrassed by. In fact, the girls LOVED it! Some of the guys became jealous of the attention I was getting, and I embraced it[9]. My circle of friends continued to grow over the years, and I became one of the most popular kids at Southeast due to my very social personality, charisma, attractiveness to the girls, but especially my intellect.

Here I was this kid from the 'hood who attracted many of the girls at school, even the older girls (juniors and seniors especially), but I also had brains to match, so to speak. Due to those long, late night study sessions with my mother at our small kitchen table when I was young,

---

[8] See photo #8
[9] See photo #9

I was always academically more advanced than other kids my age growing up.

By the time I reached high school, I was excelling in all of my Advanced Placement (AP) courses, especially the math classes, and you can only imagine how happy this made my mother. By the end of my junior year in high school, I had already taken all of the AP courses I could take at that time in 1988-89. So not only was I kinda cute, but I was also pretty darn smart as well and that resonated throughout the school and contributed to my popularity not only with the students but with teachers too.

I also participated in several of the popular classes and activities that included serving as an editor and writer on the school newspaper, participating in the Spanish Club, and being one of the managers for the boys and girls varsity basketball teams. I definitely enjoyed traveling with the teams to different schools all over the city and state, as it provided me even more opportunities to meet more girls. That was the main reason I became a basketball manager, duh!

I loved my high school years. And the more and more popular I became, the larger my circle of friends grew. And I was a bit apprehensive with this growth in the beginning, because I did not know who I could really trust. Growing up in the 'hood made you extremely selective in regards to your circle of friends and associates, as you never knew who you could *trust*. It's kind of like that line from the rappers Lil' Wayne and Drake song, "Right Above It":

> My real friends never hearin' from me. Fake friends write the wrong answers on the mirror for me. *That's why I pick and choose. I don't get shit confused. I got a small circle, I'm not with different crews.* We walk the same path, but got on different shoes. Live in the same building, but we got different views.

Nevertheless, my circle of friends was growing, but I always remained cautious. There were really only 3 friends that I consistently hung out with throughout high school and that was my long-time friend

Moe from my 'hood, Dee from another 'hood and Bone from yet another 'hood on the east side. We are all extremely popular as those three played basketball, while I focused on the ladies. Oh, don't get me wrong, they were all three just as popular with the ladies.

But Moe and I were the closest, as he and I had grown up together on the same block since we were children. And he and I would get into the most trouble in terms of 'hood-related activities – fights with other gangs in the city or any other incidences that required us to be armed, so we often left Dee and Bone behind on those escapades, as we did not want to get them involved in those type of things. But don't get me wrong, they were quick to join us for backup when requested.

Moe and I had been packing heat since middle school, so it was nothing for us to have guns and use them for our own safety and protection. And we were dumb, as we often found ourselves in places and situations where the likelihood for violence was high. What's interesting is that Moe and I were able to keep this dual life hidden from our friends at high school; the majority of them who happened to be white. I say white in the sense of these middle-class friends who had opened their doors of friendship to Moe and me and would be devastated if they knew the things that he and I would get ourselves into at times. And we didn't want to scare them off, so we just hid that part of our lives from them.

The dichotomy of our lives was definitely night and day and something that Moe and I kept secret for several years, but hid it even less after we graduated from high school.

But outside of that 'hood life during my high school years, the 4 of us were often together on Friday and Saturday nights drinking and partying and having fun with the ladies.

High school was some of the best years of my life and though I did not originally like the fact that I would be bussed to a south side school, I look back now and understand the rationale for the public school system wanting to integrate the schools. The hope would be that students from extremely diverse backgrounds could be around one another. Appreciate one another. But most importantly, respect and love one another.

But it wasn't all roses, though. As it became easier to be on the south side, my homeboys started getting upset. I made it very clear that the 'hood was home, but some still considered me a "sell-out". It was as if they couldn't understand that I hadn't had a say in the matter. That I simply did what I had to do and made the best of my situation.

I would come home after school and some of my homeboys would come up to me. They'd start taunting me and calling me a "sell-out". I'd do my best to remind them I was still one of them, that they were my homeboys and always would be. But they wouldn't hear it. Shoving would start, and before I knew what was happening, a fight would break out. This went on for a while as we all dealt with the new separation and integration that was taking place simultaneously.

While being bussed to Southeast High School and having to leave my friends behind was certainly very difficult, I did learn quite a lot. I learned that I was sheltered. I learned that I was ignorant. I learned that the media can instill a lot of false fears in people and create chaos out of harmony. I learned that if you take the time to get to know someone, you may find out that you have more in common than you think. And I learned that no matter where they bussed me, my 'hood would always be my home.

CHAPTER FIVE

THE MOVE TO MOORE

Just about anyone who hears about Moore, Oklahoma these days thinks of the massive F5 tornadoes of May 3, 1999, or May 20, 2013. But to me, Moore was yet one more tumultuous piece of my journey through the 'hoods.

It was the summer of 1988 and I was going into my senior year of high school. I'd been attending Southeast High School and finally settled in both at school and with my homeboys in the 'hood. Life was pretty smooth sailing at this point. But, as with all things, what goes up must come down. And that's just how it felt; like everything was coming down.

My parents worked hard and made many sacrifices to ensure we had what we did. Looking back, what we had wasn't much growing up. There were times without electricity, without much food, and without clothes that matched or even fit. But, my parents never stopped working to make life better for us and things did get financially better for us throughout the years.

Despite my father succumbing to more back-related issues due to his injury at work a few years prior, he was no longer able to work. He was able to receive little income through disability from social security, but what really helped us financially was that my mom would eventually land a job at Western Electric (that would later become AT&T and then Lucent Technology) as a circuit-board tester where she would go on to work for over 30 years until she retired.

Living in the rough neighborhood we did, it was only a matter of time before my parents had had enough.

We all came home one day to shattered glass and blood everywhere from someone breaking in and cutting themselves while climbing through a window. I can't remember what all they took, or what other damage had been done, but I do remember the look on my parents' faces. My father was extremely upset and was running through the house with his gun to make sure the burglars were not still in the home and my mother was upset as well crying as she just dropped to her knees in the living room. This was not the first time this happened. It was time to move.

As it turned out, my parents had been saving money over the years and preparing to move us away from the east side. Gang violence on the east side was getting worse. Looking back, it had reached its peak at this time. It was 1988 and we were living off N.E. 4th and Lottie – a very poor and rundown area even to this day. People were getting shot and killed regularly, drive-by shootings had become commonplace, and drugs were rampant. My parents wanted to escape that which had sadly become the "norm" in our neighborhood and surrounding areas. By this time, I was drifting more and more into the street life with Moe and my homeboys, especially now that I had a car. I was able to drive around and find even more trouble for us to get into.

So, my parents let us know it was finally time. We would be moving. What they didn't tell me was we were moving to Moore, Oklahoma.

Oh. My. God.

Moore is about 10 miles south of Oklahoma City. Remember, we weren't even supposed to go south of Reno Ave. which was still in Oklahoma City because that was too far south. Now we were moving 10 miles farther south?! My parents seriously thought it would be better to move away from the 'hood to the racist foothold of Oklahoma? In 1988, Moore was still pretty small and rural with only one major street (12th St.), but it was a developing community.

I knew it would be just horrible. I had reluctantly gone to parties in Moore with friends, only to be run out of town by either police or residents. All of whom happened to be white. Expletives were thrown at us such as "nigger," "monkeys," without care. This wasn't just some one-time occurrence, either. It happened on various occasions and in no way did I want to make that place my home.

One particular evening in Moore, Moe and I were pulled over. We were picking up a friend who desperately needed a ride to work. I was driving and Moe was in the passenger seat. I was traveling east on one of the main streets when all of a sudden, I saw red and blue lights flashing in my rearview mirror. It was the police. I was not speeding. We both had our seatbelts on. I had signaled when changing lanes. I had no idea why we were being pulled over but I turned off the main road onto a secondary street, as I was instructed to do by the officer on his loudspeaker. There was no traffic at all and it was not as well-lit. I got scared.

The officer came up to my window and requested my driver's license and insurance verification. I complied and provided both documents. He then requested Moe's driver's license. He provided it. As the officer was looking over Moe's license, I kindly asked, "Officer, can you tell me why you pulled us over."

"Just keep quiet, boy," was his response.

This angered me but I didn't show it, as I was *not* going to do or say anything to get us arrested, shot, or killed. I just sat there with both hands on the steering wheel and Moe with both hands on the dash. This is what young black men were taught to do when being pulled over by the police some thirty years ago, as well as today based on the current political landscape.

Moe and I watched as the officer walked back to his patrol car. He was back there for a few minutes, then out of nowhere, four additional patrol cars pulled up and had us surrounded. They got out of their vehicles with guns drawn. "GET OUT OF THE VEHICLE!! HANDS UP!!" Moe and I were freaking out at this moment and telling each other to just be cool and do exactly as we were instructed to do. So, we got out.

We were then told to lay face down on the street with our arms behind our backs and to interlock our fingers. One of the officers came and rested his foot on top of my interlocked hands which were resting on my back. The weight of his foot on my back was excruciating but I did not say a word. I could look under my car and see that Moe was in the same position I was in with another officer's foot on his back.

A couple of the other officers had been searching my car while throwing out what belongings and items were in the car. I could see these items hitting the ground and some of them even dropped on my face as I was laying there, angry and with tears in my eyes. Tears of anger and sadness.

All of a sudden, I heard a loud ripping sound and my car radio/CD player hit the ground just inches from my face. My CDs were being removed from my large case and thrown all over the ground. By this point, the officer that had his weight and foot in my back told me to stand as he said, "I want you to see this."

One of the other officers opened up my hatchback where I had this large speaker box that contained two woofers and a couple of 6X9 speakers. The police officers began to rip the woofers and speakers out of the speaker box and simply threw them on the street next to where I was standing and where Moe was now sitting.

The officers were laughing and enjoying what they were doing to me and Moe and my car. The two officers then pulled out the now empty speaker box and threw it on the street as well.

One of the officers said at this point, "Well, I guess these boys are good to go now."

We were uncuffed and I asked the original police officer on the scene again why we had been pulled over. His response while laughing at us was, "You niggers have a good night and watch yourselves." We were never told why we were pulled over. I never consented to a search of my vehicle.

After Moe and I collected all of my belongings that had been thrown on the street, as well as my broken radio/CD player, speakers, and speaker box, we simply got back into my car and drove away hoping that the officers would not find yet another reason to pull us over before making it to the highway to head back home to the east side. I hated Moore.

After being forced to go to Southeast High School as part of the integration effort, I was now going to have to spend my senior year living in Moore. The racial tensions began to grow as more black people, and other people of color, began moving to Moore. This meant more black students attending their predominantly white schools. The integration effort hadn't quite reached Moore, Oklahoma.

While I know my parents' move was an effort to better our lives, I don't think they were fully prepared for what was about to happen. Shortly after moving into our new home, they received a message on their answering machine as well as a letter in the mail. It was from the local Ku Klux Klan (KKK), ominously letting my parents know they were aware we had moved into the community. Looking back at this now, it was not too surprising, as the KKK has had a long, deep history in Oklahoma. Even walking out of a Moore convenience store, strangers would holler, "Go back home, nigger!" at me and my dad.

As my sister entered high school in the early 90s in Moore, the tension still had not decreased. You would think that by this time, there would be more acceptance and everyone would have settled. Instead, there was a "race riot" that became pretty violent between the white and black students at one of the high schools there in Moore.

Needless to say, I hated it. I hated being in Moore and did everything I could to get back to my 'hood every chance I had. I wanted to be with my friends, and was thankful for my other 'hood moms, like Mama Moe, who would welcome me into their homes whenever I could make it there - which was often! I would much rather have been back in my 'hood hitting the ground to dodge bullets from drive-by shootings, seeing the stabbings, being approached by the drug dealers, seeing prostitutes and their pimps, avoiding car-jackings and avoiding getting shot while hanging out at the east side McDonald's than live in Moore. Believe it or not, that all felt safer than being a person of color in Moore, Oklahoma in the late 80s and 90s.

It may be difficult to understand how dodging bullets could feel safer than white suburbia. But for a kid like me, I knew *why* those bullets were flying. I knew who would be after me. And I usually had a pretty good idea of when it would happen. I also knew who I could count on, which streets were off-limits to me, and so on. In Moore, on the other hand, there was none of that. People threatened my family and myself and they didn't even know me. All they knew was that we were black, we were Japanese, we were mixed-race. And for that simple fact, they hated us. The attacks were unexpected, and I was never really sure where the line between ally and enemy was drawn.

To escape the "horrors" of Moore, I spent a lot of time back on the east side, as well as with my first real girlfriend. I say "real" because I had dated many girls over the years in middle school and my freshman year in high school, but by my sophomore year, I got into a pretty serious relationship with someone I had been introduced to by a mutual friend. The year was 1987. This relationship lasted throughout the remainder of my high school years. We had great times, but there was an ongoing issue that plagued our relationship over the years. She was *white* and her parents emphatically refused to allow her to date "black boys."

This adversely affected both of us, but I believe it had a greater impact on me, as I had grown up all my life with this behavior from many whites. Please don't misunderstand me, I knew by this time that not *all* white people share these beliefs. In fact, some of my best friends, especially throughout high school, were white and their parents treated us like family.

Nevertheless, the life around my girlfriend for years was sneaking around behind her parents to meet and hang out, but we had to be sneaky and strategic. At times, she would walk down the street and around the corner from her home where I would be waiting to pick her up or drop her off. Other times, I would meet her at one of her friend's houses; have her sister or friend drop her off with me at the mall, park, or one of my friend's houses. Under no circumstances would it ever be known by her parents that she and I were together. I believe this took a toll on our relationship, as we often fought about her parents. I wanted her to tell them about me but she would not. She was scared to do so. But I continued the pressure over the years because I was getting tired of having to sneak around. Every time I was around her, I would think about our circumstances and it upset me.

My parents, on the other hand, loved and welcomed her like family. And she loved them as well, even calling them "mom" and "dad" over the years. The times we spent at my house with family and friends were always fun and joyous, but I often found myself in those moments thinking about my girlfriend's parents and why they could not accept me.

There were times throughout our relationship where I would hang out with friends and forget all about the racism and prejudiced attitudes that surrounded me in general. Then making the drive out to meet my girlfriend down the street and around the corner from her home to pick her up was a constant reminder and a slap of reality that not only infuriated me but made me sad as well. I just could not do it anymore, and I found myself doing things to push her away from me until our relationship finally ended. It was for the best. Fast forward some 30 years to 2021 and we occasionally stay in touch via social media and I am so happy for her, as she has been married for over 20 years with 2 beautiful biracial children.

Despite everything that was going on in my life with my girlfriend, running the streets with my homeboys, consumed in the gang violence in my neighborhood, etc., I still managed to graduate from Southeast High School with a 3.70 GPA, near the top of my class, yet only a 13 on the ACT. Horrible score. I figured my chances of any good college were slim to none. I was ashamed and embarrassed to tell my parents. Nevertheless, they made me apply to the University of Oklahoma (OU). Mom was still holding onto her dream of me one day obtaining a degree and becoming an electrical engineer. She wanted all those late nights of math tutoring at the kitchen table to be worth it!

I applied, and much to my surprise, I was accepted at the University of Oklahoma. Lord knows the only reason I was admitted was due to my GPA, as my ACT scores were horrid. We all celebrated my acceptance, and I prepared for the next chapter of my life. Little did any of us know what a sharp turn life was about to take.

CHAPTER SIX

SPIRALING

In the fall of 1989, I began my first semester at OU. While I wasn't exactly leaving home for college, I was still terrified and very unprepared for the culture shock, transition, expectations, and rigors of OU and college in general.

For as well as I did in high school, college made me feel like a mess. I fell behind in introductory classes and found myself struggling. High school certainly had not prepared me for the rigors and expectations of college.

I began to wonder if my high school grades had not been legitimate. Had they been inflated? Had my nomination for Mr. Spartan and being one of the more "popular kids" influenced teachers to take it easier on me? These were all of the crazy ideas and questions that ran through my mind. I know most of my teachers pushed us to do well, and I appreciate them for that, but all know is that despite my GPA and honors recognitions, I felt as if I had a lot of deficiencies and was not prepared for college.

I also believe a lot of it had to do with the transition – that is, I go from being in a high school classroom with 40 students to a lecture hall at OU with 200 students. The one-on-one attention and guidance were now lost in this sea of students.

After ending the first semester with a 1.46 GPA, I dropped out of college and would not return for nearly a decade.

My mother was devasted, and that's putting it very lightly. When I told her that I wasn't sure when I would go back, it was as if her world fell out from beneath her. She was hurt, angry, and worst of all, disappointed. She wouldn't say the words, but the look on her face said it all. I didn't want my mom disappointed in me. I felt defeated.

Anger was probably the strongest emotion I felt. I was still angry that my parents moved us to Moore. I was angry regarding the split with my girlfriend. I was angry at the racism and discrimination I had to endure. I was angry at myself. I didn't feel that I belonged in college, regardless of my mother's expectations. But looking in her eyes and seeing the longing she had, knowing it came from a place of wanting more for me, I made her a promise. I promised her I would go back to get my degree – I just didn't promise her when.

After that failed semester, I spiraled. I avoided Moore as much as possible and spent most of my time back in the 'hood. Still home as far as I was concerned, my old neighborhood provided a place of comfort and security, despite the violence and gang activity that were still prevalent.

At 19 years old, I was invincible and was fairly certain I knew all I needed to know about life. I was convinced I knew what was best for me and that nothing was going to get in my way of what I wanted. And what I wanted was to party, run the streets, and enjoy the company of girls.

I spent my nights, and most of my days, drinking, getting into trouble with my homeboys, and charming the girls. Having a girlfriend was never much of a challenge, so I had several. Ever since high school, partying, drinking, and hooking up with girls had become the norm. My long, wavy and curly hair and mixed-color skin seemed to be my ticket, as it had become this exotic fascination that spread throughout pop culture like crazy in break-dancing movies, famous music artists like Prince, and characters like A.C. Slater in the TV show Saved by the Bell.

One of the girls I was seeing, who would later become the mother of my daughter, was very interested in me and had been for quite some time, as we had known each other for years through a mutual friend. She was actually black and it was extremely rare for me to date black girls. For whatever reason, I had always been more interested and attracted to white girls at that time. You would think with my history of dating white girls and their racist parents that I would steer clear of white girls. Nope! Perhaps I was up for the challenge.

Nevertheless, we would hook up a bit more often than I would with other girls. She wanted me to settle down a bit and choose to only be with her. However, I was not in that place at that time in my life. I was still enjoying my freedom and the company of different girls, especially one that I had been spending a lot of time with over the past year or so named Tee. I don't really know what it was that fueled my promiscuity with all of these girls. There's a part of me that thinks the partying, drinking, and the girls was simply my coping mechanism to help me forget about how bad it was for me to be living in Moore.

Many of my homeboys believed it was my way of getting back at all of the white racist parents by sleeping with their daughters who were prohibited from seeing or dating black guys. But that was never my intention. At least that idea never intentionally or consciously crossed my mind. But perhaps a therapist may say otherwise.

I spent a lot of time with Tee compared to the others. She spoiled me and even though she knew I was seeing other girls, she didn't gripe or nag me about it, so I thought she was cool. However, her dad was a hardcore biker and completely fit the stereotype; owned a huge Harley-

Davidson motorcycle, always in jeans with a tucked away wallet and long chain, biker boots, leather vest with patches, and had a long mustache and beard. When he found out that she was dating a black guy, the shit hit the fan. Once again, I was not surprised.

Despite her father's feelings about me and our dysfunctional relationship, we remained together. I say dysfunctional because she knew I was still seeing other girls and never harassed me about it until much later in our relationship. But I never flaunted the fact that I was seeing other women, and I did keep some of them from her, as I was not going to throw it in her face or anything.

And if she asked about a certain girl I was sleeping with or dating, I simply denied it only because I did not want to upset her. But as time passed, I learned that she would rather know about another girl as opposed to lying to her. When she asked, I would confirm or deny, and all was good between us. As I mentioned, this was a dysfunctional relationship to say the least.

Things between us remained fairly good until a life-changing event finally put a strain on our relationship.

In the spring of 1991, I got the call that any young man of only 19 years old fears. My promiscuity had finally caught up to me. That girl, the one who wanted more, was pregnant. Oh, shit! I was going to become a *dad* before I had become a *man*! This wasn't something either of us planned, and definitely not something I was ready for. Regardless of the child on the way, I was not ready to settle down to start a family any time soon. So, I didn't.

Getting the news that I was going to be a dad, I spiraled even further. In fact, it seemed to fuel my partying, drinking, sleeping with various women, and hanging out in the streets with my homeboys, who had become even more involved with gangs. At times, we found ourselves hanging out in the hot spots on the east side. There were certain streets known for gang activity and more violence. Streets such as NE 23rd, Lincoln Blvd., and MLK Blvd. These were the areas where everyone on the east side would come to hang out, drink, cruise, etc. It was also the area most prone to heavy gang violence and violence in general.

There were plenty of times we would just be drinking, standing outside of a business, and all of a sudden, we would have to dive onto the ground as another rival gang would spray bullets at us. You could hear windows shattering behind us, bullets hitting and sparking on brick, bullet casings hitting the ground, and tires screeching as they drove off.

It wasn't uncommon for hundreds of us to be hanging out on a Friday or Saturday night. Clearly, nothing good was going to come from this many young people gathering on the east side. It wouldn't be long before suddenly shots would ring out and you would see everyone scrambling to their cars like roaches running when the light was turned on in our small kitchen at night.

Too often, after one of these gang-related events, you wouldn't just see bullet casings hitting the ground, you'd also see bodies. These weren't people hitting the ground for cover, these were people who had been shot. Victims of gang violence. Sadly, this violent reality was becoming my reality as I continued to claim the 'hood as my home to avoid and escape the city of Moore, my failures in college, the recent news I was going to be a father, and especially the disappointment of my mother.

I continued on this path of self-destruction. I had built a reputation for myself in my 'hood, as well as neighboring 'hoods as being quick-tempered, ready to react in an instant, and loyal to my homeboys. They knew if they needed me, I was always down. I was well known for not only my reputation, but for my bright red car and bumping stereo system, too, and would often roll through various Crip 'hoods. If you're not familiar with gangs of the 80s and 90s, Crips and Bloods were rival gangs. Crips wore blue; Bloods wore red. So, to drive my bright red car through a Crip 'hood, I was all but asking for trouble. However, several of my homeboys were Crips, so I would drive through their 'hoods often blasting any of my favorite rap songs.

On more than one occasion, I would be driving through and my homeboys would come running out of their houses, pulling out guns from their baggy and sagging jeans, ready to shoot up my car and me. Then they'd realize it was me and walk away shaking their heads, saying, "Oh shit, nigga, it's you! You was about to get dealt with, homeboy."

There were plenty of other times I was out either causing trouble or getting into trouble with my homeboys. From getting into fights in department stores at the mall and using cash registers as weapons, to club brawls and car chases with my homeboy "Dre" (also known as "Drego"), who was a member of the Rollin' 60s Neighborhood Crips. Dre and I had known each other from high school. He would later go on to serve time in prison from 1994-1998. When he was released, my family and I took him in and we became even closer throughout the years, like brothers. He is now a successful business owner, husband, and father. He and I still talk to this day. We always had each other's back, back in the day, so it made sense that when I got into trouble or chaos, he was usually with me.

This was simply my life during my 20s. I was out of control. Thankfully, I still had my "family" on the east side. After my time at Southeast High School, I also had my "family" on the south side. They were this amazing white family nestled in one of the roughest and poor neighborhoods on the south side surrounded by Hispanic gangs. There were many nights I would end up crashing at their house to avoid sleeping in my car, going home to Moore, or jail.

I came across this special family from a friend, Dave, I had known for years, and I got extremely close to his parents, brothers Jay and Mikey, and his sister, Tina. They lived in the south side 'hood just down the street from the "shack." The "shack" was a small convenience store owned by an elderly couple, who would sell me and Moe beer despite neither of us being old enough to legally purchase alcohol. But we tipped them well and were frequent customers, visiting them at least once and sometimes twice a day purchasing at times a box of 40oz Olde

English 800 malt liquor beer first thing in the morning. "Old-E" was what we called it and it was the alcohol preferred by gangs, rappers, and drug dealers and it literally became part of the culture during those days.

That was 6 bottles for me and 6 for Moe. Score! That usually lasted us until the afternoon and then we were back picking up another case to hopefully get us through the rest of the night, but that rarely happened. We visited the "shack" so often for years that we were trusted to have a line of credit opened there. Ridiculous I know, but we always paid our tabs.

Aside from being loyal customers, Moe and I also protected them. Their store was located in an area on the south side surrounded by predominately Hispanic gangs. The main gangs on the south side at that time that I was aware of were the Riverside Killers and South side Locos. Moe and I had our run-ins with both, but over the years there was established mutual respect, as Moe and I had known the founders of Riverside for years. We had all grown up together as kids.

As for South side Locos, my reputation proceeded itself after I got into a parking lot "brawl" with a few of their members one late Friday evening at a south side Whataburger. I will just say that after that evening, they quickly learned who I was and I never had any issues with them after that. Even when driving through their neighborhoods or stopping at the "shack."

For example, late one evening, and a few weeks after the parking lot "brawl", it was probably around 11:00 and me and Moe were leaving the "shack" after stocking up one last time for the evening. As we were putting the case of "Old-E" into the backseat, there were these two young Hispanic kids (probably 14 or 15 years old) glaring at us as they were walking past us. During this time, you didn't glare at anyone this late at night on this side of town, as you were simply asking for trouble. It was obvious that these 2 kids were in a gang as they were "reppin' their set" – that is, they were wearing the gang colors and attire that made it obvious they were with the South side Locos.

Moe and I simply blew these kids off and got into the car and shut the doors and proceeded to put the car in drive. However, we could see they had made their way to the back of the car and it appeared they were yelling something at us and either hittin' us up with gang signs or flipping us off. We couldn't really tell, so Moe and I immediately jumped out of the car and I said, "Y'all got a problem!"

One of them mumbled something to Moe as they were reaching towards their back pocket. Moe was reaching towards his gun and said, "What did you say?" And about this time, I was already reaching for my gun that was in my coat pocket, as I thought something was about to go down. However, just as I was about to pull out my gun, I heard, "MARKUS!!" I turned around and saw an older Hispanic guy across the street, and his appearance indicated he was also a South side Loco and he was running towards us with his hands up. He said, "Hey, bro, these boys obviously don't know who you guys are."

And then he yelled something at them in Spanish and the three of them walked away together. I didn't know the older guy, but a lot of the Hispanic gang members knew me and Moe, as we were often on the south side and had established a reputation not to be messed with. We were also usually recognized due to the car I drove that had these nice rims, blacked out windows, and a bumpin' stereo. Events like this were not uncommon. Just a typical evening on the south side.

My south side family had truly become a godsend. I always tell myself that they found me at a time in life when I needed them the most, as they provided food, safety, shelter, and no judgment for my behavior. They knew that I was going to do whatever I wanted to do anyway, so they would never tell me I could not drink or stay out at all hours of the night. But "moms" and "pops" always wanted me to have a safe place to stay and sleep. That's what was most important to them.

They were not rich by any means, living in a rough area in the south side 'hood, but moms and pops not only opened up their home to me and others. More importantly, they opened up their hearts to me. That's something that I will never forget, and I have always loved them for that. I truly believe I found them at a time when I needed them the most in my chaotic life, as I truly believe they helped to keep me out of jail or dead.

Unfortunately, I had lost touch with them throughout the years while I was getting my life together, and "moms" passed away in 2019. It was definitely a sad day. I went to go and see her when I found out she was not doing well, but when I arrived at the house, I learned she had passed just a few minutes before. I was devastated. I was told that during her final days she had spoken about others and me and asked for me while on her deathbed. I was looking at this sweet woman, as she lay in her hospice bed and I knew that she was truly gone and no longer in pain. That brought me a tremendous sense of peace. I held her still warm hand in mine and told her that I missed and loved her and thanked her for all she had done for me years before. Despite her already being gone, I know her spirit heard my words. I will always miss her laughter, kindness, and love.

I only wish I could have seen her before her passing, as we had lost touch for years. The funeral services were pleasant and highlighted all of the lives she touched throughout her life including mine. Pops is still alive and doing well and he and I have continued to stay in touch since moms' passing.

CHAPTER SEVEN

LOSING IT

November 8, 1991.

My home phone and beeper (or pager…Wow, I am really dating myself here) were ringing and beeping like crazy. I did not have the luxury of having a cell phone. I was trying to find them both, but in my drunken stupor, I was struggling. It was early evening, and I had been drinking with Moe since morning. I finally found the phone and with slurred speech, I answered.

To this day, I can't remember who called me. Whoever it was called to tell me my daughter's mother was in labor and my daughter would be born soon.

It was cold outside, and I was drunk. Clearly, I wasn't able to drive to the hospital. I started to get into a bit of a panic. Holy shit! I was really about to be a dad! And here I was, drunk. This was how my daughter was going to meet me.

Moe calmed me down and offered to drive me to the hospital. He probably should not have been driving either, but due to the alcohol coursing through my veins, I was not in the state of mind to be thinking rationally at that moment. To say I was nervous doesn't even come close to describing how I was feeling at that moment. I was very thankful for Moe and both anxious and excited to see my daughter be born.

As soon as we arrived at the hospital, I was confronted by my soon-to-be daughter's great aunt. This aunt raised my daughter's mom. Needless to say, she didn't care much for me at the time and the feeling was mutual. I hadn't exactly been there for her niece, as much as I should have, as she went through the pregnancy. I cared more about myself and partying than I did about what her niece was experiencing. With all of my partying, drinking, sleeping with various women, getting into trouble, and refusing to settle down with her niece, I can't say I blamed her aunt for not liking me.

That said, my daughter was about to be born, and this was not the time to get in my face. This was not the time to tell me I would never see my daughter and to be prepared to pay a lot of child support. It was not the time to be in my way.

I walked around the aunt and the nurses walked me into the room so I could view the birth of my daughter. My daughter's mom was having a c-section and I watched as the doctor made the incision. That sobered me up quick! Within just a few minutes, my precious baby girl, Jasmine, was born. They even let me cut the umbilical cord. I will never forget that magical moment of becoming a dad.

If only that had been enough to straighten me out...

Over the next three years, I *believed* I did the best I could to help take care of my daughter and her mother. For example, within the first year they moved in with me and my parents. And my parents absolutely adored their first grandchild. This only lasted a few months before Jasmine's mother had secured them an apartment.

While I still wouldn't settle down with her mother, I did find work doing odd jobs to provide what I could for her. I worked fast food, janitorial work, gas stations, anything I could find to get some money to help out. I even thought about selling drugs as the money would have been great and it would have been easy for me to do based on my drug-dealer friends who could get me started, but I decided not to because I knew it would most likely land me in jail or prison and I wouldn't be able to see Jasmine. But I seriously considered it.

I would buy diapers, formula, clothes, etc. I felt as if I were doing the right thing and being a provider for my daughter. It never occurred to me that it still wasn't enough.

While working odd jobs and partying, I made sure I still found time to stop by and see Jasmine – or "Nikki" as I preferred to call her. Her middle name is Nicole, and Nikki just felt right to me. She was a cute baby[10]. I would even occasionally stay at Nikki's mother's house to care for Nikki while her mom was at work.

I still had a "home" with my parents, but that was also still in Moore. So, I stayed where I could, when I could, with who I could just to avoid Moore as much as possible. But there were times I would make sure to stay with my parents, after Nikki and her mother moved out, so they could spend time with Nikki as well. I would often have her with me for the entire day and night to give her mother a break to relax and spend time with friends. We were co-parenting, as we were not officially "together" because I had not committed to a relationship or marriage with Nikki's mother. I was 20 years old, immature, and extremely selfish.

Even though I was now a dad and had this awesome responsibility, I had yet to change my lifestyle over the years. I felt it should be enough that I was working and providing necessities for Nikki. I didn't feel that I should have to give up my lifestyle, too. So, the drinking, partying, and promiscuity continued.

Now 23 years old, and Nikki around 3 years old, her mother had enough. In her mind, it was time for me to settle down. I had a daughter;

---

[10] See photo #10

I had responsibilities. So, she gave me an ultimatum: stop "whoring" (or sleeping) around, stop living in the streets, stop getting into trouble, and settle down and become a family or she was going to take Nikki and move away.

At that age, I didn't understand my rights as a father. I didn't have the money for an attorney. And even if I had, I'm not so sure I would have done anything about it. I just wasn't ready. I was still at a very selfish point in my life. So, in 1994, Nikki and her mother moved to Colorado. I was devastated and relieved all at the same time. My little girl was gone, but so was the added responsibility. This was the warped and twisted immature attitude and mindset I had. Sad, but it was my reality at that time.

Little did I know that this event would send me spiraling even more out of control for the next few years. Little did I know how losing it all would change my life for the better…

PART TWO

DONNING THE HOOD

CHAPTER ONE

A DAD WITHOUT HIS DAUGHTER

1994.

My daughter relocated to Colorado with her mother.

I was working full-time as an Assistant Manager at a pizza restaurant-chain to pay child support and support my social life. Late-night parties, drinking, plus lots, and lots of girls meant working full-time at a dead-end job. Being an assistant manager at the restaurant wasn't exactly going to make me rich, and it certainly wasn't a dream job, but it took care of Nikki, the bills, and kept my social life going.

Though I was still very immature and irresponsible at 23 years old, I worked extremely hard to advance in my positions at all of my jobs. Selfish as I was, I also knew that the more money I made, the more money I would have to support my social life and Nikki.

Although I wasn't ready to settle down and be a family man for Nikki, I did take my financial responsibility for her very seriously. Before she was even born, I made sure she had what she needed. That didn't stop even after her mom moved her away to Colorado.

Partying also came at a cost, and I wasn't about to lose that fun, either. So, I worked, I played, and I paid child support and provided medical coverage to make sure Nikki was taken care of.

After a couple of years of having Nikki in my life, I certainly noticed the void of her being gone. It wasn't that I didn't want my daughter around. It was that I wasn't ready to commit to one woman for life that I wasn't in love with. I missed Nikki greatly, and I was angry with her mom for taking her away. It felt spiteful that she would make such a decision to tear us apart simply because I wouldn't agree to be a family with her. It certainly didn't seem fair to Nikki.

In those times we spent together before she was relocated to Colorado, Nikki and I bonded. We had that father/daughter bond[11]. The problem was I didn't even realize how strong that bond was until she was no longer with me.

For the first few years after they moved, I was able to have Nikki travel from Colorado to visit me during some summers when she was on school break. However, these visits were usually no more than a weekend, or maybe a week if we were lucky. We didn't have a set visitation schedule, and I was naïve enough at the time, that I didn't realize I was entitled to such a thing.

When she did come to visit, we made sure to make the most of our time! In preparation for her short stay, I would take leave from work for us to be able to do several activities *every* single day she was here. We enjoyed going to the movies, shopping at the mall, playing at various parks, and sharing in my new passion: taekwondo. I made sure that we did as much as possible the entire time she was here, as I knew it would be another year before she and I would see and spend time with each other.

---

[11] See photo #11

These years were extremely sad and upsetting for Nikki. She may have been young, but the older she got, the more she was able to gain a better understanding of what was going on. She missed me, she wondered why we didn't live closer, she saw her friends with moms and dads together. She longed for us to have more time together and could see that there was tension between her mother and me.

It was during these years that there was a lot of hostility between Nikki's mom, her stepdad, and me. I was angry that she moved Nikki away; she was angry that I had refused to settle down. This resulted in having extremely limited visitation with Nikki and limited communication. Since I did not yet understand my rights as a dad, I gave in to her mother's control over my access to Nikki.

Anytime I would call Nikki, I would have to go through her mom to speak to her. It wasn't like I was a deadbeat dad. I was paying child support, covering Nikki on my health insurance, always trying to call her, and sending gifts for birthdays and Christmas. And when I say sent gifts for Christmas, I mean I would mail her a huge box that was big enough to put a Christmas tree in with several toys, gifts, and clothes. It may have appeared as though I were spoiling her, but really, I was trying to make up for the other 360 days of the year that I was not able to be with her. I was making up for all those Christmas mornings that I didn't get to watch her open her gifts, birthdays I didn't get to celebrate with her, Saturdays we should have had together where I could have been buying her little things here and there.

Being hundreds of miles from Nikki meant missing out on taking her for ice cream, talking about her day after school, helping with homework, and being her place for comfort. Sure, we could talk on the phone, but with any young child, those are not the most engaging moments. There is nothing that replaces face-to-face time with your child.

I vividly remember a time that my calls and messages to Nikki were simply not being delivered to her. When we would finally connect, she would tell me that she had never been told that I had called. This infuriated me; to imagine Nikki living her life in Colorado, thinking her dad doesn't care about her. Because, as a young child, that is the only explanation that makes sense. I was out of sight, out of mind, and I believed her mom was interfering with our ability to maintain a relationship.

When Nikki was around 9 or 10 years old, I purchased her a cell phone. My intention was to give her an independent ability to call me anytime she wanted to, as well as making it easier for me to get ahold of her as well. A few days after receiving the phone, Nikki called me in tears. I asked her what was wrong, and she told me that her stepdad had taken her phone away when she returned from a recent trip visiting me, and was not going to allow her to have the phone.

I spoke to mom and stepdad explaining that the phone was ONLY for Nikki and me to communicate and that was the sole purpose. Sure, they could add their phone numbers as well, but the phone was not meant for anything other than communication with her parents. It was stepdad who really felt she was too young to have a cell phone and was not going to allow her to keep it. I was adamant and demanded that she be provided the phone, or I would be making a trip to Colorado to settle this issue in person.

By this time in my life, I was in a much better place both mentally and spiritually. I'd had great influences and experiences which had done much to heal me, as I will explain later. Yet, I was not afraid to revert to my 'hood upbringing if I felt cornered, or that a loved one was being harmed. In this case, I felt Nikki was being harmed and 'Hood Markus was making an appearance. Come hell or high water, I was going to have access to communication with my daughter on a regular basis.

Her mother knew my history and knew that if it came to it, I would absolutely be in Colorado to handle this situation. She certainly didn't want to have to deal with all that. Let's just say Nikki was provided her cell phone later that same day. A small victory, for sure, but it was events like this that began to take their toll on Nikki. The extreme lack of visitation only added to Nikki's sadness and frustrations, and mine as well. Even at a young age, she was seeing the intent of her mom and stepdad's actions. A change was coming. And it was coming soon.

CHAPTER TWO

IMMATURE MATURITY

For many people, becoming a parent catapults them straight into adulthood. Sure, they still have their fun, but ultimately, parenting becomes their focus. This wasn't the case for me. At least, not all the way. I understood I needed to care for Nikki financially, and I was more than willing to do so. What I was not willing to do was give up my lifestyle. So, in some ways, I did grow in maturity with the birth of Nikki. In many ways, though, I remained pretty immature.

Even with all of the partying, I still had an exceptional work ethic. For as much as I was drinking, I'm thankful I never developed an addiction. I knew from watching my parents that if I ever wanted to get out of this lifestyle, I needed to remember what they had taught me through the years. I needed to remember who I truly wanted to become.

I share these events of my life with you not to give you a resume of my life, but rather to show you how, even with the adversity I lived, the poverty I experienced, and the environment I was surrounded by, I still set myself up for a future of success. It's important to me that you recognize that no matter your circumstances, you can *always* determine your own future.

I began working at 14 years old, well before Nikki came into my life. I had this innate desire to work hard and to be successful at any endeavor I undertook. Whether it was school or a part-time job, I worked to be my very best which looking back now, I attribute to watching how hard my mother worked regardless of the job.

Here I was, a kid running the streets, associating with gang members, partying, being promiscuous with the ladies…and being successful in work. My morals and my work ethic certainly appeared to conflict at this point in my life!

My first "formal" job was as a dishwasher at a large family-style restaurant inside a shopping mall in Oklahoma City. I was 15 years old. I worked extremely hard and was highlighted as one of the hardest-working employees, even out-working the adult employees at that time. I recall having to wash and clean these huge industrial-like pots that were big enough for me to get inside of. But I washed those pots, pans, dirty silverware, glasses, and washed them with every ounce of my being, because I was grateful for the restaurant to give me this job. I worked so hard scrubbing those pots and pans and dishes that I went home each night soaking wet, smelling gross, and with both of my hands wrapped in paper towels to soak up the blood from my skin being rubbed nearly raw due to the rigorous scrubbing and cleaning.

When I turned 16 and received my driver's license, I started working at a fast food restaurant for $3.50 an hour. Within only a couple of years of working extremely hard, I worked my way up to Shift Leader and eventually Assistant Manager before finally quitting for being reprimanded by the restaurant manager for yelling at an employee who called me a "nigger." Trust me, I definitely wanted to do a lot more than just yell at her.

When it happened, I caught myself clinching my fist as she was about to get slapped! But I quickly put things in perspective in that she was white and I was black and the I knew if I had slapped her, I would definitely go to jail and there would be no telling how the criminal justice system would have treated me. The thought of going to jail for assaulting a white woman had more power over me and trumped the immense anger that I felt at that moment.

While the pay improved with future jobs, so did the demands of the positions I held. Turns out, work began to interfere with my social life. Working evenings and weekends just weren't going to happen – my friends and all the girls mattered to me more than the paycheck. So, while I worked very hard to advance, I worked just as hard to get out of jobs that required me to sacrifice my social life. My mind was still focused more on playing than working.

Two years later, having graduated high school and 18 years old, I found myself working at a corporate-owned convenience store/gas station for $4.25 an hour as a cashier. Within only a couple of years, I had worked my way up to a Shift Manager and eventually Assistant Manager making $5.00 an hour. I was big time!

The following year, I was transferred out to Midwest City, Oklahoma to be the Assistant Manager at a store that needed an experienced manager to implement significant changes as the store was labeled as a "problem" store. The recent manager had just been fired, the employees were regularly known for not showing up to work, and the store was simply losing money. I was told the plan and goal was to see if I could turn the store around and if I could show corporate that I was serious and could get the job done, that I would be promoted to the Operator/Manager.

I worked extremely hard over the next year to turn that store around and I was extremely successful. However, because I did not have a college degree, I was now being told that I would not be promoted to Operator/Manager, even after all of my hard work. I was working 12-hour days, arriving at 5:30 in the morning, working all day until around 6:00 in the evening. After work, I would meet my "crew" at a friend's house just down the street to let the partying and drinking begin.

When I was told I would not become the Operator/Manager, my drive for continuing the success of the store quickly faded and I began to work less and party more.

At this time, I was the president of one of the most well-known car clubs in Oklahoma City – Low Sensations of OKC. Shout out to Chris for recruiting me a couple of years prior! We were well known for two reasons. Having really nice lowrider, custom 'rides'; and for being gang members. The perception was that any car club that had as many nice rides as we had must have had drug money or gang money to customize the rides. It didn't help that the majority of us were black or Hispanic and were known for "packing heat" (slang for carrying a gun). We simply fit the stereotype.

For some of us, "packing heat" was simply for our protection due to all of the car-jackings that had been taking place on the east side and in Midwest City as well. There were known gangs in the area.

As a car club, we could not break the gang perception, so we just *rolled* with it – see what I did there?? Rolled?? We also rolled with that perception as it helped to deter potential "jackers" from trying to car-jack any of us.

This car club provided another venue to feed my social life. I was addicted to partying, drinking, and girls. The car club provided all of those things and elevated them to a whole new level, and all of it made me feel invincible. I was popular. I was adored. People *knew* me. Everyone loved me. Rather than drugs, I focused on cars. Tricking them out, blasting the bass, racing, and cruising.

Nevertheless, we had become like celebrities, as more and more people and car clubs were hearing about us and seeing us in nationally published lowrider magazines.

My reputation especially took off when Low Sensations broke up and I became the founder, president, and leader of Reflections Car Club (the Oklahoma chapter). As you can imagine, being the face of a new car club did a lot to feed my ego and celebrity-like status, especially with the ladies. I became a leader in this group and could have kept that going much longer than I did. But there was something deep inside telling me I was meant for something better.

Over the next few years, from 1994 to around 1998, I found myself working as a Shift Manager at a nationally-owned restaurant chain, working my way up to Assistant Manager in 1995, and then Restaurant General Manager (RGM) by 1996. Once again, I had an unbelievable drive and work ethic to be the best, something that I know I inherited from my mother, but unfortunately, my social drive was just as strong up until about 1997-1998.

By this time, I was known by the restaurant chain group of owners in Oklahoma for having the ability to completely transform an underperforming and failing restaurant into one of the top-producing stores in my area and region. In only my first 2-3 years as an RGM, I was able to transform 3 failing restaurants and was still managing all 3 at the same time for well over a year. I was doing the job of a higher-paid Area Manager, but without the official title, salary, and benefits. Why? Because I did not have a college degree. UGH!! Here we go again! I was devastated and very angry.

It's 1998. I am 27 years old. I was hit with the news that I would not be promoted to Area Manager despite doing the work. I had been working extremely hard to better my financial situation so I could provide more for Nikki who was in Colorado but was denied that opportunity due to a lack of a college degree. I had grown tired over the years of having this as a reason or excuse not to be promoted for all of my hard work.

I was still out partying and drinking, but nothing compared to the previous years, as I was on a mission to change my social-economic status and financial well-being. I was missing Nikki terribly because in the past 4 years since she had relocated to Colorado her mom only allowed me to see her perhaps 2 or 3 times in those 4 years, and when I did see her, I was lucky to have her for a weekend only during the summer. I will be honest here. I could have raised a fuss about it with her mom, but I did not, as I was too focused on partying and running the streets, and working as an RGM. It was convenient but extremely selfish on my part to some extent.

CHAPTER THREE

MEETING THE POOS FAMILY

In the summer of 1998, something happened; something that would be life-changing and impact me for the better. I enrolled in a martial arts program.

Poos Taekwondo has been teaching martial arts, self-defense, and the Olympic sport since 1975. They are internationally known and have had numerous Junior National Champions, Senior National Champions, Collegiate National Champions, Olympic medalists, and Olympic Coach affiliated with their school over the years.

I vividly remember walking into Poos Taekwondo in northwest Oklahoma City for the first time and being greeted by a young, blonde-haired, tanned, white guy who looked like a model straight off the cover of a Guess, Hollister, or American Eagle magazine. I had called and spoken to him about taekwondo classes the day before.

I said, "I'm here to see Jason Poos."

He smiled and said, "I'm Jason, and you must be Markus." I replied with a confused, "Uh..." I couldn't help but think to myself, *What? Where's the short Asian guy that I had expected to meet with the last name Poos?* Jason could see the confusion on my face and said, "I get that all the time." Our friendship was born.

The Poos family resided in Edmond, Oklahoma which is one of the wealthier cities in the Oklahoma City Metropolitan area. Edmond is known for its 5-star schools, affluent neighborhoods, and amenities: nice parks, good streets, high-end restaurants, and retail stores, etc. Though some label people who reside in Edmond as "snobs", "uppity", "arrogant", "elites", etc., the Poos family could not have been more different. This was a close family bonded by their love and their love poured out to anyone that came into contact with them and I was no exception.

I envied the Poos family, but not in a resentful manner – that is, I was jealous of them and the closeness they still had with each other and their 3 sons who were all pretty close to my age. I was jealous to learn of their upbringing. Though they were not raised "rich" by any means, their upbringing was a lot better than mine. What I saw in their *family* was how I wish my family could have been as well, but we were dealt very different cards in life, so to speak.

Within the first few months that I spent with the Poos family, especially Mr. and Mrs. Poos and their sons, Jason ("Jae") and Justin ("Judd"), I wanted to gain their approval, not only as a martial artist but as a man. Here I was 27 years old, working paycheck to paycheck at a restaurant chain with no future aspirations, running the streets, no college degree, having a daughter that I rarely saw, and depressed. I'd look at these sons who had college degrees, owned businesses, and had nice homes and cars.

There was something about this family that motivated me to want to be a better man, and I can tell you that a lot of it was the love and caring nature they had for me. I mean, when I first walked through the doors and met Jae, I was still dressing in baggy jeans, oversized t-shirts, exposed tattoos, and wearing multiple gold rings and necklaces. I was the epitome of "ghetto" and still had that ghetto-thug mentality. But that mentality quickly changed. After a few weeks, the Poos and their entire extended family of Taekwondo showed me I had nothing to prove. I didn't need to show up as a thug to get respect and take my place in the room. In fact, I learned it was the exact opposite.

A lot of people from the 'hood have this mentality that they have to dress "hood" or "ghetto" to show others that they are "hard" and down to whoop your ass if you cross them. In a way, it's a mentality that *demands* respect from others as opposed to *earning* respect from others.

Most people who first saw me saw a thug. They expected a hardened exterior, gangster talk, and a no-care attitude. But with the Poos family, there was no judgment. They simply welcomed me. That 'something' I felt inside myself yearning to be more. The Poos saw it, too, and they nurtured it. I still had my family, but with the Poos, I had more. They had everything I longed for, and they were willing to mentor me so I could achieve. The Poos knew I was more than baggy jeans and gold chains.

After a few months of training with the Poos, my mentality and attire went through a major overhaul; but only when I was around the Poos family. When I was back in the 'hood, or around my homeboys, I reverted to my ghetto-thug mentality and still reppin' with my hood attire. I didn't want anyone thinking I'd forgotten where I came from, or that I was now somehow better than them. They were still my family, too, and I didn't know how to make this transition without losing respect in my 'hood.

I do not know if the Poos family knew this at the time, but I found this family for a reason – kind of how I felt with moms and pops on the south side. There was something bigger than us that brought us together. I truly believe that. But there were other people and families at Poos Taekwondo that embraced me with that same love as the Poos the minute I walked through the doors of the school. Some people that especially stood out and immediately befriended me were Adam ("Bue"), Aaron, Charity, Ron, Salar, Darya, Jason ("Bones"), Trevor ("Homer"), Sauman, Stuart ("Beef" or "Bofart"), Luke, Michael, Tessa, Seth, Jenn-Daye, and others, as well as families that included the Farrows, Nevilles, Naismiths, Faizais, Days, Smiths, Lallis, Floyds, Stranges, Thorpes, Lambrechts, Esches, Kaneshiges, and countless others.

Just 2 years after first walking through the doors of the dojang, attending multiple classes every day, and working extremely hard on mastering the art of Taekwondo, I earned my first-degree black belt (Kukkiwon Dan certificate) in 2000. This was no easy task, as the average time to achieve the black belt is about 3-4 years. At this point, I had received my first-degree black belt faster than one other person had ever done in the Poos program, and they had been in business for 25 years at that time.

I had drive, determination, and love for the martial art. That love extended to the Poos family, as well as the overall taekwondo families. I knew I was already part of the martial art family, now I wanted to be a part of the "black belt family" as well. It was a brotherhood that you could not easily be a part of. You had to earn it. And I did earn that right, as my work ethic in reaching that goal was a relentless, non-stop approach that included attending multiple classes every day, 6 days a week, working tirelessly for hours at home every single day as well. I was addicted to taekwondo. But looking back at things during that time, what I was addicted to was the sense of family and especially the *peace* and *discipline* that taekwondo and the Poos family and extended families and friends provided me at a time in my life when I needed it the most.

Just four years after walking through those doors for the first time, I stood as one of the groomsmen in Jae's wedding, I house-sat for Mr. and Mrs. Poos while they went on vacation, and I was invited and involved in a lot of their family functions. I became part of their family outside of taekwondo, and they became part of mine.

I invested in this family more than my own immediate family. In other words, I invested more of my time and emotions with the Poos family because I felt this need to and wanted to, as they had pretty much embraced me like part of their family. I actually felt that I had become closer to them during this time than my own family (mom, dad, sister, and nephew). I mean, I was spending significantly more time with the Poos family and the extended Poos families than I was with my own parents. I was with or around the Poos family and the extended families literally 6-days a week, whether that was taking taekwondo classes, training with the elite team, or just hanging out for lunches or dinners on the weekends with them.

It became a lot easier to spend more time with the Poos family, especially due to the problems that I had had with my father over the past few years. He and I clashed about all sorts of things but it primarily had to deal with my actions in life around that time: occasionally coming home late at night drunk with girls, as I lived with my parents until I was like 26 or 27; no college degree; no career; partying all the time; and so much more. He and I clashed so much that it led up to another and final physical altercation and that was the last straw for the both of us. And I finally moved out and moved in with Tee.

My mother was completely devastated. She begged me not to go, as she slowly walked up to me and rested her forehead on my chest and crying profusely as she and I were standing just outside of the house. It absolutely broke my heart, as I NEVER EVER wanted to hurt my mother, but the damage had been done, and I had no choice but to leave because I could no longer remain in the same house with my father. And I believe it was best to leave now before things escalated and got worse.

When I reflect back on how things just clicked with me and the Poos family, it was because they offered and provided me a loving "home" at a time when I needed it the most, which was something that I felt I had lost due to the strained relationship my dad and I had for years that led to my departure.

For the next 10 years or so, I became a permanent fixture at Poos Taekwondo, becoming an employee, one of the lead instructors, earning my 2nd and 3rd degree black belts, and becoming one of the trainers and coaches for our nationally and internationally recognized elite team of competitors.

I absolutely loved coaching all of the elite athletes, but it was the trust that the Poos family had in me to coach these athletes, as the Poos name resonated throughout the Taekwondo world and it was expected that a large number of our elite fighters – Team Poos – would be placed on the U.S. Taekwondo teams based on the history of our success.

I mean, taekwondo is a violent sport and you can be seriously injured or knocked out in a split second, and the stakes were extremely high at any national competition in regards to how you finished or placed (gold, silver, or bronze) as it affected your seeding once you get to the National Championships. There was definitely a lot of trust in me, and I appreciated that and truly became a student of the sport.

One of the highlights of my coaching was when Team Poos was in San Antonio, Texas, I believe, for the U.S. Junior National Championships, and I coached one of our elite competitors all the way to the gold medal which also meant that he would represent the U.S. on the Junior National Team. During these same championships, I also coached one of my "lil' brothers", Salar, and got him to the semi-finals (medal rounds), which was the first time he had reached this level in all of his years competing up until this point. Proud moments right there.

I also mentored, trained, and sponsored several candidates to prepare for their black belt test that included: Jennifer, Heather "Meldrum", Tessa, and countless others as my way of giving back to the program. Being a sponsor for a black belt candidate was no easy task, as you have to dedicate a lot of your time and energy over several months in preparing them for the rigorous 3-hour black belt test. But sponsoring a black belt candidate was simply a way of giving back to the Poos program and I loved being requested by several candidates each year to be their sponsor despite my intense and rigorous preparations and extremely high expectations.

But around 2010-2011, I could no longer dedicate as much time to taekwondo anymore due to other endeavors that were demanding more of my time and energy (work, daughter, education, etc.). Through their mentoring and friendship, the Poos family really helped me close doors and move forward like a man and father. They helped me to erase my ghetto image and mentality so I could truly become all I was capable of being.

I truly enjoyed my years at Poos Taekwondo and with the extended families and friends at Poos that I still keep in contact with today. These years were life-changing and I will forever be grateful to all of them.

CHAPTER FOUR

BE BETTER, DO BETTER

In the fall of 1999, I finally decided to go back to college. I was at a point in my life, at 28 years old, that I finally realized that I needed to get myself together. I had been consistently partying and drinking for years and running the streets, and I had just recently buried my cousin and uncle who both had been killed in separate "gang-related" incidences. Their deaths were the aha! moment for me to get off these streets and go back to school.

Being at my uncle's funeral, especially, and watching his little girls and son crying because they would never be able to spend time with their daddy again absolutely broke my heart. And I really began reflecting on my relationship with Nikki. And I did not want her to have to attend my funeral well before she and I had years to spend special moments together.

Nikki was the main motivation for returning to college as I believed that an education would open doors for me, especially financially.

Something that was ingrained within me by my mom at such a young age, as she and I had those late-night study sessions at our kitchen table. So, going back to college was also for my mom. I knew it had always been something extremely important to her. She had been disappointed in me ever since I dropped out back in 1989. She *never* told me she was disappointed, but I could see it in the tears in her eyes when she learned of my failing semester and that I was not going to return.

Ten years had passed since I dropped out of college, so when I returned in 1999, I was on a mission to make up for that lost time. And I say "lost time" because I felt I had wasted 10 years of my life running the streets, partying, drinking, dating several girls, working dead-end jobs, not being a good dad. Going back to college was not easy by any means, but I was focused and in a different place mentally, this time around.

I was definitely on a mission to complete my Associate's degree, as I knew it would either help in my transition to a 4-year institution or serve as a quick reminder that I did not have what it took to succeed in college. I am not going to lie, I was afraid. I was afraid I would not do well. But more importantly, I was afraid of disappointing my mother again.

But I remember walking up to the front doors of the college on my first day of classes, and before opening the doors, I took a deep breath and said to myself: "You got this!" And I walked through those doors with this sense of confidence and determination that I would not fail again.

I first attended Oklahoma City Community College in the fall of 1999 and was majoring in political science-pre law. I had aspirations of going to law school and becoming an attorney to be able to represent those back in my 'hood who could not afford quality legal counsel. I had seen so many people in my neighborhoods and other poor communities suffer without affordable representation. It was also during this time that I was starting to assist and unofficially teach other students at

Poos Taekwondo, and I loved that role as well. Little did I know how much these teaching experiences would influence my future.

I felt a little out of place during my first semester, as I was normally the oldest student in each class. I was 28 years-old while the majority of students were roughly ages 16 to 20. However, I was able to hide it very well, as I looked a lot younger than I was, something that I have been blessed with my entire life. It's the Blasian (Black/Asian) genes I received from my parents. As the sayings go: "Black don't crack, and Asians don't raisin."

Every once in a while, my age would finally come out during class discussions or something when mentioning having an 8-year-old daughter to everyone's dismay and shock. A lot of my professors were even shocked, but it also made sense to them, as my demeanor and the way I communicated, according to them, was beyond the typical student they normally had. And many of them praised me for returning back to college.

I shared a little of my background and experiences during some class discussions – well, none of the poor or especially bad stuff of course – but I vividly recall something special that happened in my English Composition I course taught by one of my favorite professors to this very day, who is now retired.

One of our major assignments in the class was a reflection paper where we had to reflect on a significant event that occurred in our life. The professor had no idea of my upbringing or anything. Being that we would not be sharing this reflection paper with any of the students or presenting the paper in front of the class, I felt comfortable reflecting a little bit about my struggles in life and what led me back to college after 10 years.

And I knew the professor would not judge me or anything based on my experiences with him in class over the past few weeks. He was this really sweet, old man, who always made it a point to say good morning to me each day. He was always very soft-spoken and it created this feeling or sense of calm when you were around him.

We submitted our first drafts to him on a Friday. On Monday, he said his usual "good morning, Markus", while gently pulling me to the side and asked if I would stop by and see him at the end of class. Oh shit! I thought I had really done something bad now.

I had all of these crazy thoughts racing through my mind: was my draft that horrible, was he going to tell me to drop his course and take some remedial course because I was not writing at a level susceptible to being in his current course, did I not follow his guidelines for the paper, and so much more.

I was a complete mess for that entire 50-minute class. Class ends and I walk up to his desk and say, "you wanted to see me, sir." He begins to tell me that he read over my draft and it was the best draft in the entire class and one of the best drafts he had ever read. My eyes start to tear up.

He goes on to tell me that my story was definitely a compelling and touching story and that he was extremely happy to see me back in college. As he stated, "Welcome back, Markus. Welcome back." And at that time, I just sort of fell into his arms and cried. I had finally felt that I belonged and felt such relief as if this huge weight had been lifted off of me.

And he had been so impressed with my final draft a few weeks later that he requested to allow him to publish it in some type of English department paper/article for all students and professors to see. That was definitely one of the best highlights of my academic career.

I ended my first semester attending full-time (4 classes or 12 credit-hours) with a 3.69 GPA. All A's and one B in General Biology, but who likes Biology anyways. I was definitely disappointed because of that B.

Well, I did not take that much time to celebrate my academic achievement, as the upcoming semester was only about a month away. I was definitely proud of myself, but I was on a mission to continue this push to be the best student I could be, while also reminiscing about those late study sessions with my mother at our kitchen table. Her spirit was definitely with me on this academic journey. And I continued to push to get one step closer to my academic goals.

My second semester was fairly easy as I was taking mostly elective courses. However, my third semester was a beast! But it would be this semester in which I would meet a professor who would have a significant impact on my life and become one of my mentors even to this very day. And that professor was Dana Glencross.

Professor Glencross taught the Introduction to Law course and based on what the majority of other political science majors had told me, I better stay clear of this course and take something else instead, as it was not a required course for the degree. But I was up for the challenge. I wanted a professor who would push me academically, as I knew it would only better prepare me for a 4-year college or university.

Boy did she not disappoint! She had a background in the fields of Political Science and English and attended law school. She was brutal in the classroom and reminiscent of Viola Davis's character in the TV show: "How to Get Away with Murder." Professor Glencross did not play and expected disciplined and focused students in her law class. As that is what is expected in law school, as many political science majors plan to go on to law school. By her attending law school, she was able to bring her experiences and perspectives into her course at the community college. And I LOVED IT!!

Despite Professor Glencross's stern demeanor, she was a very supportive professor, who always encouraged us to come and visit with her if we had questions, needed additional clarification in regards to an assignment, or if we needed some type of personal legal advice or direction.

She was a very open and kind professor once you got passed that first week or so of the course because she knew that if you stuck it out a few weeks, then you were a serious and dedicated student, and you needed to be for this course.

I often found myself in her office to look over one of my briefs that I would be submitting and presenting to the class soon. She always took the time to visit with me as she knew that I was driven to be a good student, but I also wanted to be one of her best students as well.

The more and more I visited with her, the more she learned about my upbringing, challenges, and motivation to come back to college. She was touched by my story and I believe over time became more invested in my success, not only just in her course, but with my life in general.

Though her course was one of the most rigorous courses throughout my academic career, I appreciated her for challenging and motivating us to be the very best students and human beings we could be. Oh, and I made an A in her course and was deemed one of the best "Moot Court Teams."

Professor Glencross definitely made me a better student and I felt I was now better armed, so to speak, to take on any course, so I took another one of her courses and did well in it, too. She continued her mentorship of me and really prepared me for what to expect at the university levels. She would sit down with me to go over my admission letters and scholarship applications.

She was someone I had really bonded with and trusted and that was something extremely difficult to do – that is, I did not trust a lot of people and my circle of family and friends was small.

Little did I know at the time that Professor Glencross's approach to teaching and mentorship would be instilled within me, and my own students, years later, would see a lot of her spirit resonate through my teaching.

I took everything that I had learned from Professor Glencross into what would be my final semester and final political science course. And boy would I need it! The course was the Introduction to Political Science. And it never felt like an introduction course by any means, as it was taught by Professor Jim Johnsen, who first appeared as this very arrogant, condescending, intimidating, loud, and outspoken person.

Though he was in late 50s or maybe even early 60s, he looked like he was in his early 40s, as he was this very fit man and you could tell he worked out on the regular, as you could see his biceps bulging through his dress shirts. He was very intimidating.

I had been forewarned about him by other political science majors just as I had been warned about Professor Glencross. The difference between Glencross and Johnsen, however, was that Johnsen's course was required for us to obtain a degree in political science (pre-law). I had no choice but to take his course. But I was prepared. I was ready. Professor Glencross prepared me for this.

Professor Johnsen did not disappoint and lived up to all of the horror stories that a lot of us political science majors had heard about. However, he was very much like Professor Glencross in his demeanor, approach to teaching, and challenging us as majors. I absolutely loved his class.

And the other students in the class did as well – that is, those that stuck it out. Those that could not keep up with the pace or his expectations quickly dropped the course and changed their major to something like Liberal Studies or Diversified Studies. But for me, that was the easy way out. I wanted the challenge.

Just as we had experienced with Professor Glencross, Professor Johnsen was extremely dedicated to the success of his students. You could see his passion and more importantly, you could feel it during his lectures when at times his voice was so loud that other professors stopped by and poked their heads into our classroom to make sure everything was okay.

He was not screaming or anything, but his voice just resonated as if he was this opera singer on stage belting out this high note. But for Professor Johnsen, the classroom was his stage. He was just this very vibrant and passionate professor and you loved and respected him for that. And he often took the time to meet with me regarding coursework, my plans after the community college, and just things about life in general. He and I definitely bonded and this bond would later grow into a very good mentorship, as he continues to be one of my mentors to this day.

As we were trudging through this rigorous course, we learn from Professor Johnsen that our class would be his last. WHAT?! During one of our final classes together with him – let me remind you that for the majority of us in this final political science course, this was also one of our final courses period, as we would be graduating at the end of this semester – he notified us with tears in his eyes that he was retiring at the end of that semester. He shared with us that out of his lengthy tenure (25 years+) as a professor and teaching this required course, that we were the absolute very best of the best and he felt that it was only fitting that he retired with his best group of political science students. Aww.... this news was sad, but it was also uplifting as I was coming to the end of my studies at the community college.

Even years after his retirement when he moved to California, we would talk on the phone and he would always bring up how we were the best class he had ever had. And when he visited me and former colleagues, he would always bring it up again. He was very proud of us. I do not bring this up to brag or anything, I bring this up because you could always hear the joy and happiness in his voice when he would say it. Our class provided him that peace to retire and knowing that he had done great things throughout his tenure and with us.

I respected the hell out of that man and truly appreciate the foundation that he provided for us to succeed in our academic studies, but also in life. Little did he know he would also instill within me his spirit of teaching. And many years later, I found myself taking over and teaching his Introduction to Political Science course and bringing that same vibrance and energy that he once carried into the course. He was definitely proud of that moment.

In May of 2001, I graduated with a 3.88 GPA with my Associate in Arts (A.A.) degree in political science, having received only two B's in all of my classes. I was extremely disappointed with the two B's in General Biology and Principles of Microeconomics but was proud of myself nonetheless. So was my mom. I did not like those two courses anyway and could not find anyone else who liked those courses either.

Despite falling just short of a 4.0, I received some recognition and awards based on my academic work.

My experiences at the community college were priceless. I truly believed that a lot of my professors, especially the ones like my English professor, Glencross, and Johnsen really prepared me for that next step in my academic journey, and I did not want to disappoint them despite the stigma and stereotypes attached to community college students. Let me explain.

There has always been, even to this day, this stigma and stereotype that community college students are basically just a little smarter than they were when in high school. In other words, community colleges basically teach as if we were simply in the 13th-grade, so to speak, and we had not really been academically-challenged nor proficient in the higher levels of learning that is expected and found at a 4-year university.

Well, I wanted to kick down that ignorant door and misperception and wanted university students to know that I had the academic and intellectual background and preparation to stand side-by-side with any of them. And I wanted their professors to know as well.

I was definitely channeling my 'hood mentality, as I was always taught to be a fighter growing up and to hold my own with anyone. I fought bare-knuckles in the streets with gang members. I have been shot at by gang members. I have been in knife fights with gang members. I have been involved in full out brawls in clubs with gang members. University students and professors were not going to scare or deter me from my goals and my journey.

I had this chip on my shoulder when pursuing my next step in my academic journey. But I also had this pressure not to disappoint my mentors back at the community college who expected so much of me, as I was a product of their teachings, and I knew those at any university would look at me to judge and determine whether I fit the community college stereotype.

In the fall of 2001, I transferred to the University of Central Oklahoma (UCO) in Edmond, Oklahoma where I was continuing to pursue my degree in political science. I stepped through those doors with guns a blazing, as I had something to prove. And it did not take very long for other political science students and professors to recognize that I was driven, focused, and very disciplined.

And you should have seen the shock on students and professors faces when they learned that I was a "community college student." I am telling you, this stigma and stereotype was really a thing. I excelled in all of my courses, whether they were my major political science courses or in my minor fields of study: criminal justice and sociology.

What I also learned was that I was actually more advanced in my knowledge, writing, and research skills than most of my peers, especially within political science, and I had my professors and mentors at the community college, especially Glencross and Johnsen, to thank for that.

With every semester that passed, and the more I excelled, I was becoming more and more popular throughout the political science department and caught the attention of a few of the tenured professors, who would also take me under their wings and mentor me.

Though I absolutely loved all of the professors in the department, there were three in particular, who really mentored me and became like family, and that was Dr. Brett Sharp, Dr. Greg Scott, and Dr. Jan Hardt.

Anyone you speak to would describe Dr. Sharp as this "teddy-bear-like" individual who was just so soft in terms of his demeanor and voice. He always had this very happy attitude and it just consumed you as well. Not only was he this great scholar, but the way he carried himself in and out of the classroom with students never made us feel inferior or anything to him.

He and I quickly formed a bond that continues to this day. He's always been one of my biggest supporters and there is no way that I would have been able to achieve the things I did during my tenure at UCO without his guidance and mentorship.

Dr. Scott, on the other hand, was this very stoic and relaxed person, who spoke with this sort of New England accent with a very deep and serious voice that made you feel like you were in the presence of royalty or something. But he had this very high-pitched squeaky laugh that instantly made him appear to be normal. Nevertheless, he was still this great scholar and educator that everyone knew him to be. And when you add in his slicked-back, bushy-like grey hair, that looked as if he had just jumped off a surfboard after riding a huge wave, you were even more intrigued by him.

Dr. Hardt was definitely someone who helped me navigate throughout my studies, as I had taken a few of her political sciences courses that were required for my degree. She expected nothing but the best from us and was quite stern in her expectations, but she was also very kind and sweet outside of the classroom. She and I worked a lot together when I began pursuing my graduate studies as she was the graduate advisor and co-sponsor of the political science honor society. She was always a supporter of my journey.

I definitely bonded with Dr. Sharp and Dr. Scott more and they had become my 'hood moms, so to speak, as both of them were extremely instrumental in my success at UCO and beyond. I became part of their family as they opened up their homes to me for lunches, dinners, and so much more.

Even several years later when Dr. Scott had retired, he gave me a special gift while at dinner with him and his lovely wife, Dr. Jill Scott – may her sweet soul and big heart rest in peace. He gave me his academic robe that he had once earned and had worn for years to several graduation ceremonies at UCO. And now he was passing it on to me. My heart just sank and the tears flowed, as he and I just embraced each other at that moment. He was such a great man and continues to be a part of my life today. Though we don't talk as much as we once did, I know that I can pick up the phone any time and call him and it would be as if no time had passed.

During my tenure at UCO, as I previously mentioned, Dr. Sharp was one of my biggest supporters in that he was always recommending that I submit my research papers in hopes of being published, encouraging me to moderate and present my research on the death penalty at several student-led symposiums, encouraging me to step up and be an officer and later the president of Pi Sigma Alpha (the political science honor society), and so much more. That's how much faith he had in me.

And he always praised me for any of my successes in and outside of the classroom. For example, if you go to his office today, he still has an autographed, framed, 8X10 photo hanging up on his wall of me on the cover of a martial arts magazine[12]. He was so proud. And, at times, I hear him telling other students and colleagues about me when they ask him who that guy (me) is on his wall that is surrounded by all of his academic accolades and awards. And he tells them that I was a former student that did a lot of great things for the department during my tenure there and that he's expecting to see me hit the big screen one day with my looks and skills. I love that man!

My journey in obtaining my Bachelor's degree was a great experience. Looking back on it, it definitely reminded me of "the Village" that looked after my sister and I and others in our poor neighborhood grow-ing up – where everyone in that community helped to take care of each other and I found that neighborhood/village again with several profes-sors (i.e., Dr. Shawna Cleary, Dr. Sid Brown, and others) throughout UCO, but especially in the political science department.

In December of 2002, just a year and a half after receiving my A.A. degree, I graduated with my Bachelor's degree in political science (with a minor in Criminal Justice) with a 3.78 GPA making either the Presi-dent's or Dean's Honor Roll every semester. I found myself taking 18 hours during some semesters, as I was on the fast track to obtaining my degree. I chose the fast track because I felt I had wasted 10 years of my

---

[12] See photo #12

life after dropping out of college previously. So, in only 3 years, I obtained my Associate's and Bachelor's degrees. According to research and data, the average time for a student to obtain their Bachelor's degree is around 5 years.

I am not gonna lie, it was extremely challenging and there were times when I thought about just giving up. But I could not give up. If I gave up, I would be giving up on my dreams of being able to take care of Nikki and provide the things that only I believed a degree would afford me.

What I shared in these previous paragraphs may sound as though I am flaunting my success. That is not at all my intention. Where I grew up – how I grew up – didn't typically lead to successful lives for the youth of the area. But, where and how you grow up do not have to define you. People who thought I would never amount to anything, who said I would end up in prison or dead, who expected me to fail…I didn't let them win. In fact, I made a very concerted effort to prove them wrong.

No matter your beginnings, you always have a choice to be better and do better. To find a family to make your own, and to get yourself out of the 'hood if that's what you desire. There is absolutely nothing holding you back other than yourself – and a whole world ready to help you to become the very best version of yourself. Had I succumbed to my environment, to societal expectations, I would have fallen victim and very well may have ended up in prison or dead. But that wasn't the way I was going to allow my life to proceed. And those who cared for me would not allow that to happen either.

It was also during these rigorous academic years when pursuing my degrees (1999 to 2002) that I found myself stressed and depressed due to Nikki's mom only allowing me to see her during the summer and only for a handful of days if I was lucky. Nevertheless, I was still driven to pursue my degrees despite the additional stressors.

CHAPTER FIVE

STUDENT AND TEACHER

After Nikki's mom left for Colorado in 1994, I rarely got to see my daughter. Her mom did her best to make me feel as though she was in complete control of any communication I had, whether that be by phone, or in person. I had no idea what rights I had as a father during these years. I was young and uninformed. I mean, I was 23 years-old when Nikki left for Colorado and had no idea I had rights as the father, despite not being married to Nikki's mother. I simply believed, and even some older men that I have spoken to over the years also believed, that the mother had all of the rights in regards to the child(ren).

That's why I never challenged or fought with Nikki's mom regarding the limited visitation. The last thing I wanted to do was to upset her mom out of fear that she would not allow Nikki to come and visit at all. So, I stayed in my lane, so to speak, and never made it an issue.

I desperately wanted to spend time with my daughter. I wanted to be her father. The years leading up to her relocation to Colorado in 1994 were much different than where I was now. I was in a much healthier place mentally and spiritually. This healthier me wanted to spend as much time with Nikki as possible, and she wanted that as well.

It was 2001, and Nikki and I were preparing to travel to Dallas, Texas for one of the major Taekwondo competition events; the Junior Nationals Championships. In the previous years, when she was down visiting me, I got her involved in taekwondo and she loved it! She instantly made a lot of friends within the Poos Taekwondo family. Nikki was extremely excited to be able to take this road trip with all of us and see many of her friends compete at the national level.

This particular summer, I was allowed to have Nikki for about a week or so which was long enough for us to attend the Junior Nationals event. However, the day before we were to leave for Dallas, Nikki's mom contacted me to let me know that Nikki could not attend because mom wanted her to spend time with Nikki's cousins, who also resided in Oklahoma City. I was told that even if I chose not to attend Junior Nationals that I still could not spend time with Nikki and instructed to take her to her cousin's house. Of course, I was livid. I was simply going to ignore such instructions from Nikki's mom, keep her, and attend Junior Nationals anyways. But after speaking to a very close friend, who was also a family attorney and a part of the Poos extended taekwondo family, I dropped Nikki off at her cousins' and vowed to have this fight another day. In court that is.

Nikki was devastated and crying the entire time during the drive to her cousins' house. And she could not understand why this was happening. Why was she being required to spend time with her cousins and not her dad?

The last straw came in the Summer of 2002. When I arrived at the airport to pick up Nikki, who was 10 at the time, she was in tears and crying hysterically. I knew she was only going to be visiting me for about a week, but something in my heart was telling me that was not going to be the case. I asked her what was wrong and she told me that for the week that she was going to be in town visiting with me, which is the only time I saw her each year, that she had to go and spend a few days with her cousins. This ultimately meant that my week had now turned into only a few days. I was beyond upset and I found myself falling to my knees and crying along with Nikki as we held each other.

A few months later on Dec. 11, 2002, with the assistance of my attorney friend, we filed a motion to implement a standard visitation schedule. Before filing the motion, I told my attorney that I did not have the money or assets to pay him for his services. He said to me, "Don't you worry about it. You're family, and Nikki is part of our Poos family as well. And we take care of our family." These were the type of people I found myself surrounded by within the Poos Taekwondo family. I was extremely grateful to him, as submitting the motion for standard visitation was just the start of something much bigger.

I had no idea until speaking with several friends and my attorney that as Nikki's father I was entitled to standard visitation rights. Going to court would ensure that I had Nikki for my share of holidays and school breaks.

Just two days after filing the motion to establish standard visitation, I graduated with my Bachelor's degree. I was also accepted into the Master's degree program at the University of Central Oklahoma majoring in political science with a minor in Criminal Justice. I was anxious and excited to begin classes for the spring semester. I was determined to get through this program quickly, as well as excel. I always wanted to do more than just finish, I always strived to finish strong.

Based on my academic performance within the political science department, I had gained a reputation that piqued the interest of several full-time professors in the department. So much so that I was asked to be the Graduate Assistant (GA) for the political science department. This was huge! Only one student from a select few are ever requested to be the GA for the department, so it was an overwhelming honor and privilege to serve in this role. The role provided validation for all of my hard work regarding my academic studies over the previous years. It also served as a reminder that there were high expectations of me by the department, as I needed to continue to remain disciplined and focused with my academic studies while also managing the responsibilities of being the Graduate Assistant, teaching part-time as a black belt instructor, dealing with the visitation battle regarding my daughter, and so much more. But, hey, I was 32 years old at that point, so I had this!

Some people wondered why I was pushing so hard to receive my political science degree. What initially motivated me was the idea of eventually going to law school to represent those back in my 'hood who could not afford an attorney. However, that path took a drastic and unexpected change. Sometimes life has a way of hearing your desires and then deciding to throw a crazy curveball at you.

It was the spring of 2003, and I was in my first semester as a full-time graduate student, as well as the Graduate Assistant for the political science department. My sights were still on law school. However, there was a full-time, tenured professor who was on his way out to retirement and I was asked by the department chair to shadow and assist this outgoing professor, Dr. Thompson. I was excited but extremely nervous, as I didn't know what Dr. Thompson expected of me.

I attended his first lecture of the semester and was completely blown away. Unfortunately, not in a good way. His lectures primarily consisted of the things he did over the weekend, his personal life, and nothing to do with the Government course. When he did discuss items related to government, it was at times incoherent, not on topic for the lecture scheduled for that day, and confusing. I felt frustrated for the students and would often look out into the classroom to see the confused and dazed looks on their faces, but I was just the Graduate Assistant so I stayed silent for the most part while witnessing the confusion that unfolded in front of me.

I wasn't sure if it was my place to report what I was witnessing. Nevertheless, I went and voiced my concerns with the department chair, Dr. Scott.

When I met with him regarding my concerns with Dr. Thompson, he immediately let me know that other students had come to voice their concerns with him as well. We had a plan that would be respectful to Dr. Thompson, while also allowing me to play a slightly larger role as a Graduate Assistant. The plan was at the end of some of Dr. Thompson's lectures, I would take a few minutes and provide a "brief summary" of the lectures to the students. Of course, we (Dr. Scott and I) would need to run this by Dr. Thompson. Turned out he was perfectly fine with this new plan, as it meant less lecturing for him to do.

The following week, as Dr. Thompson was finishing up yet another confusing and unrelated topic lecture, I used the remaining 10-15 minutes of that class to provide a summary and answer questions. At the end of that week, Dr. Scott had called me into his office. I thought, *Oh, man, what did I do?*

When I peeked into his office door, he asked me to have a seat and then explained to me that several students came to see him again and requested that I provide my summaries, and answer questions at the end of every class. Dr. Scott agreed that I continue to do this as well. I was honored and excited, but more importantly, I was happy for the students.

Dr. Thompson did not care about me providing my summaries at the end of each class and after the next couple of weeks, he gathered his belongings and returned to his office while leaving me alone with the students and I *loved* it! As each week passed, the earlier and earlier Dr. Thompson would leave me with the students to provide my summaries which were slowly turning themselves into full-blown lectures. By about halfway through the 16-week semester, Dr. Thompson was no longer lecturing and would stay in his office and work. He often thanked me, as this allowed him more time to work on other school-related projects. His government classes were pretty much handed over to me. My teaching career was born!

Teaching seemed to come naturally to me. I had been teaching for the past few years as an instructor at Poos and they did not let just anyone teach. I had to master the material. More importantly, I had to teach it in a manner that was easy to absorb, while also being personable, caring, and trustworthy. I have always said that to be a great teacher is to have a *gift*. And this gift transcends anything that you can be taught out of a book or learn in a class. Those students who are reading this right now know exactly what I mean about this gift. Some teachers and educators have it; some do not.

I discovered that I had that gift. That gift of teaching that piques the interest and facilitates dialogue and discourse among group of students who could care less about government and politics in American Government courses. That gift that made them critically think about the world and how we treated or mistreated one another without a fight breaking out in the class. That gift that made government and politics actually fun!

I cannot tell you how many thousands of students over the years have shared with me via student evaluations, emails, or in-person how fun I made an expected "boring government class" actually fun. I guess it was not boring after all, and I also learned from them that I was not teaching the course in the same "boring manner" like most of the "old-timers". And this is within the context that the majority of students who take any American Government course absolutely do not want to be there. They are only there because they are required to complete the course as part of any degree in Oklahoma. Sad, but true. My philosophy was that if they were going to be stuck with me, I might as well make it fun while learning the basic principles of our government.

My first semester as a graduate student and GA in the political science department was interesting, but more importantly, that semester, along with teaching as an instructor at Poos helped me to find my true calling. It turns out that law school wasn't the trajectory I was meant to be on after all. I wasn't a lawyer, I was an educator.

While I was managing all of the responsibilities delegated to me during this time, I was still battling with Nikki's mother regarding the standard visitation schedule. There were many nights that I cried myself to sleep as I wanted so badly to be spending more and more time with her. She and I would both cry on the phone at times, as she was missing me just as much, if not more. I promised her that things would work themselves out. A mantra that I still tell others today who need a positive outlook.

Just two months after I filed a motion for standard visitation, Nikki's mother attempted to fight the standard visitation schedule. She didn't want to share holidays, nor did she want to use her benefit of flying Nikki for free through her job as a flight attendant. She appeared to feel as though I should be responsible for all expenses since I was requesting my rights be honored. But the judge was "not having any of that nonsense." These were standard requests, per a standard visitation schedule, and they were non-negotiable as conveyed by the judge.

By summer of 2003, I was appearing before the judge again at another hearing to finalize the standard visitation schedule. I could see the judge's frustrations mounting as we progressed through this standard visitation hearing. But in the end, the judge ruled in my favor. Despite the stressors of having to appear before the judge to argue my case for standard visitation, this hearing, and its records would eventually serve as evidence in a much bigger court hearing yet to come.

Although Nikki's mom did her best to make the process as difficult as possible, Nikki and I prevailed through the court. This was huge! This changed our lives and provided the boost in energy and motivation I so desperately needed to continue my academic journey. Throughout the court battle and rigors of school, I compartmentalized the best I could. I still managed to graduate with my Bachelor's degree, along with receiving several undergraduate awards.

Over the next year and a half, I worked diligently to obtain my Master's degree. I had already fulfilled my promise to my mom, but I wanted more. Knowing I wanted to teach as a professor, I knew I needed a Master's degree. So, I pressed on. Nikki and I also got to enjoy our first year together, getting to see each other much more often than we were used to. Keeping busy with school helped to fill those gaps of time in between our visits.

I like to think that Nikki helped to propel my academic journey. I wanted to stay busy when she wasn't with me, so I immersed myself in my studies. This garnered my excellent grades and additional accolades. Just having Nikki in my life on a more regular basis had me in a much better place both mentally and spiritually. She became my motivation as well as my inspiration.

Little did we know at the time that this one victory of newly acquired and additional visitation we had been awarded in court would bring even more changes for us in the not-so-distant future. Great things were on the horizon for Nikki and me.

CHAPTER SIX

REUNITED

Nikki and I had been spending more and more time with one another since the court order establishing standard visitation back in June of 2003. One afternoon, I received a call from Nikki. She was 11 years old at the time, and very mature for a child that age. We discussed how much happier we both were. She and I further discussed the issues she had been having with her stepdad – issues that trace back to when Nikki first met her stepdad when she was 4 or 5 years old. Nikki and her stepdad had always had a rocky relationship, so this discussion was just one of several discussions throughout the years. It was not something new.

Since relocating to Colorado back in 1994, Nikki had always had issues with her stepdad. When I was able to talk to Nikki during those days, she would tell me things that I chalked up as a little girl who was simply missing her "daddy". But as the years passed, the stories and her relationship with her stepdad never really changed for the better. Since her mom was a full-time flight attendant and gone most of the time, Nikki was often left with just her stepdad and half-brother and sister.

There was no abuse or anything like that regarding her stepdad, it was more a matter of him being a strict, unfair disciplinarian. According to Nikki, her stepdad treated her very differently when compared to the son and daughter he'd had with Nikki's mom. And over time, I was seeing that as well.

I cannot recount the number of times Nikki and I discussed this, and at times I found myself reaching out to her mother to voice my concerns as well. My only communication, in the beginning, was primarily through Nikki's mom and not the stepdad, as I wanted to be respectful, and that line of communication had always been the norm for years. I knew if I spoke directly to him that I would most likely get upset and make my way to Colorado to do something that would make things worse.

So, in the early years, I kept the communication lines open to just Nikki's mother. But, of course, that changed over time, as I found myself hearing more and more from Nikki during our phone calls, or when she was in Oklahoma visiting, about what she and I perceived to be unfair treatment and a consistent negative attitude towards her.

Over those years, the stepdad and I had several heated conversations which led to both Nikki and her mom begging me not to come to Colorado to deal with stepdad, as it would only make things worse. Nikki and her mother knew how "ghetto" I could still be if I needed to be. You know that saying: "you can take the thug out of the ghetto, but you can't take the ghetto out of the thug." Yep, that was me! And with a black belt, too.

Nevertheless, in May of 2004, Nikki and I were having another conversation about her and her stepdad, and the discussion quickly turns to Nikki wanting to come and live with me permanently. The previous year or so of us being able to spend more time together only solidified the fact that Nikki wanted to be with her daddy. This was not the first time this discussion had come up. Over the years, Nikki had always asked to come and live with me permanently. These conversations, of course, came after her relocation to Colorado when she was only 3 years old. So, from the time she was 3 years old until she was 12, we probably had 20 or more conversations regarding her coming to live with me permanently.

However, there were two main reasons I would always tell her that now was not the time. First, I was not ready to be a full-time dad. I had a very selfish attitude, I know, but some of it was due to financial reasons. Second, I felt that Nikki was too young to objectively make that decision, and I did not want to drag her through a court battle. I knew it would be an ugly fight.

Now here we were, having this conversation again, a few weeks before graduation for my Master's degree and just a week or so before she was already scheduled to come and visit for the summer. But several things were very different this time regarding whether to move forward with a custody battle. I had some financial stability working as a temporary, full-time faculty member at the University of Central Oklahoma, as well as being an adjunct professor at Oklahoma City Community College. I had finally reached some level of maturity and had a healthier outlook on life. But most importantly, Nikki was not a young child anymore. I believed she was finally old enough and mature enough at the time to decide to come and live with me permanently.

During our phone call, I told Nikki once I started the process there would be no turning back. I finally asked her if she was absolutely positive that she wanted to come and live with me permanently and her answer was, "Yes, daddy. I'm ready!" I responded with an agreeable, "Let's do this!"

You see, despite my immaturity during the early years of her life, Nikki still saw how hard I fought to see her. To talk to her. To spend more time with her. I never missed a birthday call or sending large boxes of toys and clothes every Christmas or any other special occasion. Oh, how I would have loved to Facetime, Zoom, or even Skype, but those platforms were not available back in the early 1990s and 2000s.

Limiting the time Nikki and I could talk or see each other, only made our relationship stronger, as she was always a daddy's girl. She and I always had this bond and I believed it was the result of her mother and stepdad's actions that helped to strengthen it. Even at an early age Nikki recognized this and brought it to my attention several times over the years. She was very bright and mature even for a child her age.

My next phone call was to Nikki's mother to notify her that Nikki had made the declaration that she was ready to come and live with me permanently. This should not have been surprising to her mother, and it wasn't. Even though Nikki had voiced her opinion and desires to live with me several times over the years, it turns out her mother had never taken those feelings seriously. While she wasn't surprised when I told her about Nikki's choice, her mother still got extremely angry and felt betrayed by Nikki. I went on to provide some of the reasons for Nikki's decision, namely that Nikki was stressed, depressed, and was tired of her stepdad's treatment of her over the years, and being kept away from me for years. I ended by saying that I believed it was in Nikki's best interest at this time.

I asked Nikki's mother to discuss and confirm these things with Nikki, as I wanted her to hear it from Nikki herself. A few hours later, Nikki's mother called and shared that she and her husband discussed things with Nikki and they agreed to let her come and live with me permanently. I was so excited!

Nikki called me in tears of joy shortly after my phone call with her mother. She was equally excited. Though this was amazing news, it would be short-lived.

Over the next year couple of years (2004-2006), things were great! Nikki had moved to Oklahoma to live with me permanently. She started middle school, gained a ton of friends, and she was able to visit with her relatives that were here in Oklahoma, especially the ones who had monopolized her visitation time with me years ago. She and I were both happy. She was finally home.

Here I was, a newly full-time dad, working full-time, and now I learned I had been accepted into the Ph.D. program in the political science department at the University of Oklahoma (OU) to begin in the fall of 2004. I knew joining this program was most likely a horrible decision based on information I had been given, but I felt I didn't have a choice, as it was the only Ph.D. program in political science in the state at the time and even now, I believe.

Despite the challenges I encountered at OU in the preceding years, which I will discuss in more detail in the following chapter, I will say that the spring 2006 semester was also challenging and exhausting because Nikki's mother had filed a motion a few weeks prior to Nikki returning to Colorado for summer visitation with her mother. Nikki's mother was now arguing that Nikki's living arrangements with me were "temporary" and for only one year and never something that would be permanent. Here we go!

My attorney presented the argument that IF the "agreement" was that Nikki would be living with me "temporarily" – or for the summer of 2004 through summer 2005, then why did Nikki's mother send her back to me after visiting with her mom and family at the end of the summer of 2005? It's now spring 2006!

If the agreement between Nikki's mother and I were simply based on her two arguments (temporarily and only for one year) filed in the motion, then she never would have returned Nikki to me in August of 2005, so she could start her second year of middle school in Oklahoma. Boom! Mic drop!

There would be several motions filed with the court over the next few weeks but to no avail. We were going to court to settle this custody dispute once and for all. I was ready – or, at least I thought I was. The stage was set.

It was 8:15 a.m. on Monday, Feb. 13, 2006. Nikki is 14 years-old. It was a very cold and gloomy morning with temperatures near freezing. I remember this morning very vividly, as it was a life-changing day for me. I made sure that Nikki was bundled up and warm with her winter coat, scarf, and gloves. We were both excited but also terrified as we did not know what this day had in store for us. We held hands as we walked across the street to enter the Oklahoma County Courthouse. I remember swooping her up into my arms just before we got to the curb, as the street was slick with ice and I did not want her to slip and fall. She was laughing a little as it was fun for her to be swooped up like I had done so often when we played when she was little. Inside of myself, however, I was not laughing or having fun. I was crying a little bit but hid it from her as I held her close in what turned into a hug. I was scared. I was weak. I was a mess. But I did not want her to see me like this, as I needed to be strong for both of us. I did not want her to have to consider the consequences of today which would be her having to move back to Colorado.

My good friend and attorney, who had been with us for this entire journey, met Nikki and me in the foyer of the courthouse. He hugged Nikki and told me to take her upstairs to the library where she would wait until the judge was ready to have her come down and testify. I walked Nikki upstairs and into the library where there was a small area with a table and chairs, puzzles, and games. I gave her one last hug and a kiss and she looked at me and said that "everything is going to be alright, daddy." She could sense that I was worried, but I held strong at least during our hug. But as I walked away, I could feel another tear running down my cheek.

I gathered myself and walked downstairs and met with my attorney and we waited for the court clerk to call us into the courtroom. What felt like hours was only a few minutes and we were summoned. When I took my seat next to my attorney, I could see Nikki's mother and her posse that included her husband, aunt, uncle, and attorney all seated on the opposite side of the courtroom talking and laughing with one another.

Their apparent confidence and arrogance that they would win this custody hearing only fueled my anger which is what I needed to snap me out of the sadness that I felt since waking up that morning. I was now ready to fight for my daughter. Let's do this!

"ALL RISE!" The judge entered the courtroom and took his seat, and then we all took our seats. Nikki's mother and her witnesses all testified and were trying to plant a seed with the judge that the only reason Nikki wanted to live with me permanently was that I was some sort of pushover dad. That I let Nikki do whatever she wanted to do without any restrictions, consequences, or disciplinary actions on my part. This was of course BS and nothing more than a common tactic. My attorney and I fought back to show that my parenting role was that of fairness but with discipline as well. You see, I let Nikki spend the nights with her girlfriends, go to chaperoned parties, go to the movies with friends, stay up late at home on the weekends, etc. – all things that teenagers experience and should experience in their lives. Nikki was not a little girl anymore. When she came to Oklahoma in the summer of 2004 to live with me, she was 13. So, yes, I allowed her to do these things, not because I was some pushover dad, but because she was a mature and responsible teenager and earned the right to do the fun teenage things due to her grades and mostly good behavior.

Nikki's grades were mostly A's and B's. She never got into any trouble at school and when I attended her parent-teacher conferences, all of her teachers had nothing but great things to say about her. Nikki was on the basketball and track teams. She was in the show choir. She was also a mentor to other students at her middle school.

Every parent I had ever come into contact with at one of Nikki's school events always spoke very highly of her. Nikki rarely got into trouble, but if she did, it was typical teenager stuff that mostly revolved around her attitude. *All teenagers have attitudes*. But best believe she was disciplined, whether that meant she would be grounded or even worse that she would have her phone take away. She would rather have her teeth pulled than be without her phone. But, "she gon' learn today" as comedian Kevin Hart would say.

I never had to spank Nikki even though that was what she was used to with her stepdad back in Colorado. All I ever needed to do was call her by her first name: "Jasmine" and she immediately knew she was in trouble. I am not judging parents who spank their kids because trust me, I got my ass beat by my father with belts, shoes, or anything else that was within reach. While I was certainly prepared to physically discipline Nikki if necessary, I just never had to resort to that. Nikki wasn't a perfect child, but she listened to me and was good about learning from her mistakes.

So, my attorney and I explained all of these things to the judge. My attorney also highlighted the fact that when Nikki brought home her first and only C in middle school, I grounded her from her phone, from going over to her friend's house, and had her sit out a few basketball games and a couple of track meets. I was clearly not this pushover parent that let Nikki get away with poor grades or bad behavior despite what Nikki's mother, husband, aunt, and uncle had testified to.

On the contrary, I was a disciplinarian. I never considered myself a strict disciplinarian. Just a fair disciplinarian. I saw how some of Nikki's girlfriends were sheltered and kept locked up all of the time and prohibited from going to parties, the mall, movies, or other places of entertainment with friends. And these were the same girls who were sneaking out of their homes late at night when their parents were asleep. These were the same girls that experimented with drugs. These were the same girls that got pregnant at 14, 15, and 16 years old. Times had not changed; I saw the same girls growing up in my 'hoods that got into all kinds of trouble with very strict parents. I learned enough throughout my own life and experiences that I wanted to find a good balance of being a fair disciplinarian.

What I learned was that with fairness comes honesty. Nikki saw the fairness I provided her through my disciplinary actions. And she owned her mistakes. But more importantly, my parenting attitude always provided a safe place for her to come and talk to me about anything. She was never afraid to discuss even the most sensitive issues like drugs, alcohol, sex, and boys, as she had witnessed many of her friends consumed in those things.

We could talk about these things because I was not unfair and overly strict. I was a disciplinarian, but I was fair and open to discuss anything. She never needed to sneak out of the house because I allowed her to attend chaperoned parties. She never needed to lie to me about boys because she and I talked about the boys she liked. She never needed to experiment with drugs because she and I talked about drugs, their harmful effects, and possible consequences, and she saw firsthand how it adversely affected her friends.

This was the type of relationship that I had always established with Nikki through my role as her father. And this is why to this very day that she has always been closer to me than anyone else.

This was just some of the testimony that I was providing to the judge that morning. And after hours of providing testimony, being questioned by my attorney and Nikki's mother's attorney, we had finally come to the part during the trial when it was time for Nikki to provide her testimony before the judge as for the reasons why she wanted to remain living with me in Oklahoma.

However, as the judge was gathering his notes, he leaned back in his chair and stated that he had heard everything that he needed to hear and was not going to call Nikki down to provide her testimony. What?! I was shocked, as I believed her testimony would compel the judge to allow her to remain in my custody. I was in complete disarray. However, Nikki's mother, attorney, husband, aunt, and uncle were all extremely happy with laughter and were high-fiving and hugging each other and had to be silenced by the judge. They truly believed the actions of the judge by not calling Nikki down to testify meant that she would be returning to Colorado soon.

As I was trying to collect myself, I got up from my seat and started to head out of the courtroom since we were now in recess. As soon as we were out of the courtroom, my attorney could see the confusion, sadness, and exhaustion passing through my entire body. I asked him point blank, "What does this mean? Why is the judge not going to have Nikki testify?" He was shocked as well and could not determine if this was a good thing or a bad thing.

You see, I believed that I absolutely needed Nikki to testify, as this was not a normal custody case in my mind. In other words, especially in Oklahoma, as long as a mother wasn't addicted to drugs, in prison, posed a danger to the child, the courts overwhelmingly placed the child with the mother. And I believe this is why Nikki's mother and her posse were so excited when we all learned Nikki was not going to testify. I was very concerned that Nikki was not going to testify.

As my attorney and I were deeply locked into our conversation in the hallway, we were abruptly interrupted by the very loud celebration of laughter and more high-fives and hugs among Nikki's mother and her posse across the hall from us. This angered me. But I was mentally and physically exhausted as well due to the hours of testimony and cross-examination. So, we simply waited.

If I recall, it was a little after 1:00 p.m. What seemed like several hours of waiting had only been about an hour or so before we were called back into the courtroom for the judge's final ruling. Here we go.

The judge began providing his ruling and was speaking in this legal language that I could not comprehend. I was very confused. I was clinching the notepad and pen provided by my attorney at the onset of the trial. I was sweating. My heart was racing 100 miles per hour. The judge continued. In desperation, I leaned over to my attorney and whispered, "What is the judge saying? I do not have a clue of anything he is saying."

My attorney grabbed his notepad and wrote something on it. He discreetly slid it over to me. *YOU WON!!* I nearly cried out with joy and excitement but had to keep my emotions in check so as not to disrespect the judge and the court. It's really difficult for me to put into words the emotions that were going through me as I looked down at the notepad still fixated on those two words: *YOU WON!!*

Just reflecting on that moment as I am writing and sharing this with you brings tears to my eyes, but nothing like the tears that ran down my face as I was trying to remain quiet and still as the judge continued to provide his ruling. I just sat there being still, my heart still racing, while reflecting back on all of the wrongs that I believed Nikki and I had been subjected to over the years. But I continued to sit still and listen to the judge's words.

"It is further ordered, adjudged, and decreed by the Court that Defendant be and is hereby designated as the primary custodial parent." Those were the words I was so patiently and desperately waiting to hear from the judge. But the judge did not stop there, and here is where I was provided some validation for all of these years of fighting for the right to spend more time with Nikki.

The judge awarded all of my attorney fees to be paid by Nikki's mother. Furthermore, the judge then looked over to Nikki's mother, as I recall, and said something to the effect that she should be lucky that I was only asking for joint custody and to be the custodial parent, as he would have awarded me full custody had I requested it. I recall he scolded her for her actions going back to challenging my standard visitation motion back in 2003; only allowing Nikki to see me a few days out of the year for years; arguing that Nikki's living with me was temporary despite contradicting testimony from her husband; and so much more.

It was evident he was not amused by her actions or the testimonies provided by her husband, aunt, and uncle. This was reminiscent of the other judge that also got irritated with Nikki's mother back during the June 2003 standard visitation hearing.

I sat there in that courtroom and just continued to look down at that notepad while listening to the judge. I was now just waiting to hear his gavel strike the block to make that resonating sound that would signal that we were done and that Nikki would officially remain in my custody. And then it happened…BAM! We were done.

I was so emotional that my attorney had to help me up from my seat. I was crying profusely, and he and I just hugged each other. He was holding me up at that point, as my body somewhat collapsed into his due to the overload of emotions. I was crying and thanking him so much for everything that he had done for us. We continued to embrace one another and he then said to me, "Go and tell Nikki. I am sure she would like to know that she will be staying in Oklahoma for good."

I thought, "Oh shit!" I was so overwhelmed and caught up in my emotions that I had completely forgotten about Nikki, who was patiently waiting upstairs for me. I rushed off to tell her the great news.

As I ran up the stairs, I was still overwhelmed with emotions and crying. As I reached the library doors, I scanned the room and found Nikki seated at a table reading a book. I ran to her in tears. She saw me crying and then immediately started crying as well. As I got to her, I picked her up and gave her the biggest hug while still crying. I was so emotional that I couldn't speak. She was crying thinking that we lost and that she had to return to Colorado.

I finally gained some composure and told her, "You are staying with me! The judge ruled in our favor." She and I began to cry even more at this point. We were so overrun with emotions that we just sat on the floor. She was so happy, and so was I. After a few minutes, we composed ourselves and made our way downstairs to the foyer where my attorney was waiting for us.

As soon as Nikki saw him, she ran over to him and gave him a great big hug. She started crying again and so did I. After a few minutes, we collected ourselves and finally made our way outside and began walking across the street to my car. The sun was finally out and it was now a bright and beautiful day.

As Nikki and I crossed the street, I heard, "Markus!" I turned around and see Nikki's stepdad. He checked the traffic and then crossed the street to make his way over to me and Nikki. He reached out his hand to shake mine and said, "Congratulations, you won." I told him that this was not a competition for me and it never had been. This was all about what was best for Nikki and I left it at that and shook his hand.

At this time Nikki was waving goodbye to her aunt and uncle and asked me if she could go and say goodbye to them. I said, "Of course." I was not bitter with anyone anymore. I had been validated. Nikki was now able to permanently live with me and I never had to worry about her mom trying to take her away from me. All was right in the world, and things would only get better for us.

For the record, shortly after the trial, Nikki's mother, stepdad, aunt, and uncle had complete changes of attitude towards me. I don't know if it took the trial or my actions afterward, but all of the hostility disappeared. We have all been really cordial with one another for years, even going to dinner and hanging out over Nikki's mother's and stepdad's home when visiting my grandson in Colorado. I never thought it would happen, but I am so very glad it did.

Just a few months later in July of 2006, I was offered a full-time position as a professor of political science at both Seminole State College and Oklahoma City Community College (OCCC). The job offer at OCCC was really made possible by my mentor, Professor Dana Glencross, who really advocated for me to the hiring committee. The decision was easy. I accepted the job at OCCC. At the age of 35, I finally had a career with benefits and retirement.

I say "career" as opposed to a job because I have always believed that a job is something you are forced to do, even if you don't like it and at times feeling like you are just clocking in and out. A career, on the other hand, is something you wake up to each morning and go in and put in your hours without it feeling like a job. When you are shocked at the end of each month when you see that direct deposit paycheck hit your account, because you are doing something you love and it does not feel like work, you, my friend have a career. Just my thoughts.

This full-time position as a professor was a major step in my life, as I felt it had finally provided me with some sense of stability to take better care of Nikki and my family[13]. I was so excited after accepting the full-time position that I took my parents, Nikki, my fiancé, Melissa, and her six-year-old son, Dylan, out to dinner at Nikki's favorite restaurant where I surprised everyone with the great news.

Of course, my mother was extremely happy and proud of me. I went back to college and got my Associate's, Bachelor's, and Master's degrees and now had a full-time "adult job" as she and I had jokingly put it. But most importantly, my mother was proud of me. I fulfilled my promise of going back to college for her and was not done just yet in pursuing more advanced degrees. That family dinner was definitely a special one.

---

[13] See photo #13

CHAPTER SEVEN

ROAD TO DOCTOR

A few weeks before graduating with my Master's degree in 2004, a couple of my mentors requested a meeting with me. These mentors, Dr. Scott and Dr. Sharp were more like family to me, as they not only mentored me since first stepping foot on campus at UCO in the fall of 2001 but, more importantly, they treated me like family throughout my time at UCO by providing advice and love that went well beyond just my academics. They truly cared for me and were fully aware of how far I had come in my life at that point. Even to this day, they are very much a part of my life.

I arrived at the meeting which took place in one of the offices in the political science department. Upon entering, I saw my two mentors; Dr. Scott and Dr. Sharp. No big deal. Until I turned to the right and saw the Dean of the College of Liberal Arts seated as well. Uh oh!

The dean was aware of my exceptional academic standing in the College of Liberal Arts, as he was the one who often handed out awards and plaques, and he handed me several at the recent awards ceremony.

I took my seat and the meeting commenced. The dean then asked me if I had ever considered pursuing a Ph.D. out of state at an Ivy League college. The dean, Dr. Scott, and Dr. Sharp, all well-known and respected educators and scholars, truly believed that based on my academic standing at UCO and in the political science department, I would be better served attending one of these institutions, as opposed to pursuing a Ph.D. at the University of Oklahoma.

They believed that an Ivy League degree would definitely make me more marketable regarding a future teaching position in higher education.

They also believed that not only could I handle the rigors and expectations of a Ph.D. at any of those universities, but they knew that I would excel and work through any of the challenges that degree would throw my way. I was shocked and humbled by their kind words and the belief they had in me. In a way, they believed in me more than I did myself.

I thanked them for their kind words, but also let them know that I was not in a place financially to be able to attend one of those universities as the tuition, housing, books, and other costs were well beyond my means. There was absolutely no way that I could afford to attend any of those universities, even with scholarships. Their response was simple, we would find scholarships, grants, and perhaps UCO, the College of Liberal Arts, and the political science department could also put together a scholarship for me to help supplement any of the other scholarships that I may receive. They were determined. And I was still in shock. They gave me hope, a belief that perhaps I was good enough, and that this dream could be possible.

However, beyond the financial constraints of attending one of those universities, I had just recently found out, via verbal agreement by Nikki's mother, that Nikki was going to be living with me permanently, and there was no way that I would relocate her to the east coast after convincing her mom and stepdad that it was in Nikki's best interest to live in Oklahoma. I did not want to complicate things or give them a reason to fight me to return her back to Colorado. Besides, there would be no way that I could be the father I wanted to be for her while also trudging through a rigorous Ph.D. program at an Ivy League school. It would not be fair to Nikki nor my studies. So, I did what any father would do when faced with this dilemma and it was simple: I gave up my dream to attend Harvard University for a bigger dream which was to be a full-time father to Nikki.

When I broke the news to the dean and my mentors, they were disappointed, but understood my circumstances and knew that I had made the right decision. University of Oklahoma (OU), here I come! But not without its challenges. Luckily, I had been forewarned.

Before applying to the Ph.D. program in political science at OU, I was forewarned by several friends, professors, and mentors regarding the political science department and its programs at OU. What was commonly mentioned was that that department was a very "elitist" and "egocentric" department, especially since they were the only institution in the entire state that offered a Ph.D. in political science. So that department truly believed that you better walk through fire for them.

It was also divulged to me that as a graduate student, you better devote your entire LIFE to that department by spending all of your time in teaching and research. You better "fit" into their "club" or you would not last very long in their program. Lastly, there were a couple of professors in particular that I was told to avoid if at all possible. But I thought, hey, I am a 33-year-old man and could handle any challenges that came along with that department. I survived the 'hood, so I could survive this department. Boy was I wrong.

I was accepted into the very competitive Ph.D. program in the political science department and began my studies in the fall of 2004. However, a few weeks before the start of my first semester, I received a phone call from the department secretary. She was requesting that I drop off some forms for the upcoming semester. So, Nikki and I headed down to Norman, Oklahoma to do just that.

I dropped off the forms and as I was about to leave the office, the secretary let me know that Dr. Plato wanted to meet with me. They had heard so much about me and were excited to have me. I knew this department was extremely selective in who they admitted into their Ph.D. program, so it did not surprise me that they were aware of who I was. As I walked into Dr. Plato's office, they asked me to have a seat. I had Nikki sitting just outside the office. Dr. Plato went on and on about how they were very impressed with my curriculum vitae (or academic resume). So much so that they would like for me to be their GA. This was one of the professors that I had been forewarned about regarding the challenges of the department, but here I was in their office and they were offering me a prestigious and sought-after job.

I respectfully declined the position, but not solely because I wanted to stay as far away from this professor as possible. It had more to do with the already high expectations and demands for my studies. There was no way that I could balance Ph.D. studies, be a full-time father, work, and be a Graduate Assistant for Dr. Plato. I would be stretched too thin and did not want to put myself in a position where I would be letting someone down, whether that would be Nikki, Dr. Plato, my professors, or myself.

Dr. Plato's reaction to my decline struck a nerve, and I could see the veins popping out of their forehead and their tone of speech instantly changed to a sterner voice. This professor went on to tell me how they were one of the leading professors at the university who brought in millions of dollars in grants each year or something to that effect. They also went on to tell me how they were also one of the most recognized professors in the department, the university, and the state. This professor was not shy at all about boasting about themselves. Furthermore, Dr. Plato went on to tell me that out of all of the graduate students each year that they only selected one that they thought was *worthy* of the position and that I should reconsider my decision.

I told them I was extremely honored and humbled by the offer, but based on my circumstances, I regretfully had to decline. Dr. Plato stood up to shake my hand and that is how the discussion ended. As I walked out of Dr. Plato's office, I felt right then and there that I now had a target on my back and would be blacklisted. But I will let you be the judge.

I already had strikes against me going into the political science department at OU. I was a non-traditional student. That is, I was in my mid-30s while the average Ph.D. students were in their mid-20s; I was teaching as a temporary full-time professor at UCO, and teaching part-time as an adjunct professor at OCCC, while most of the other Ph.D. students were working part-time as graduate assistants, research assistants, or as an adjunct professor; I was raising a child while none of the Ph.D. students I knew or were aware of had any children; my life was consumed by my daughter while the Ph.D. students' lives were consumed by the political science department and all of its demands.

I was definitely not in the "clique" with the political science department or its graduate students, Ph.D. students, or Carl Albert Fellows. It was no secret, and I was treated that way by all that were a part of that program. Still, I continued to endure and push through, but it was not without its challenges.

The next year had its ups and downs. The ups were definitely that Nikki was now living with me permanently, but the downs were dealing with the recent breakup with Tee, as we finally ended our 14-year relationship, as she and I had simply grown apart over the years. I was not the same person she first met when I was 18 years-old. She was really good to me over the years and put up with a lot of my BS, even helping me raise and be a part of Nikki's life. She and Nikki are still really close to this day.

I was also dealing with challenges I faced with a certain professor. The fall 2004 semester went well. The spring 2005 semester went well, too. The fall 2005 semester was a mess! I made my first C in my graduate studies. I had made all A's during my entire graduate studies at UCO and some of the courses that I had completed here recently at OU, so I was not happy at all with this C which is pretty much equivalent to a failing grade at the graduate level.

As graduate students, in most graduate programs, you are only allowed to receive 2 grades lower than a B throughout your entire graduate studies before you are withdrawn from the program. And here I was with a C in a class that I had already completed its equivalent at UCO.

I completed a graduate course at UCO that transferred and substituted for the graduate course that I received a C in at OU. However, before taking the course at OU, the professor, Dr. Jones, who was also on my Ph.D. committee, requested a meeting with me before the start of the semester. He *strongly encouraged* me to take their course despite having already completed the course at UCO. This was not surprising as the political science department at OU felt that their courses were superior to any other university that offered the same. So, even though I received an A in this course the previous year at UCO, I was sitting down with this OU professor who was now pushing me to take their course. They mentioned that it would be a "great refresher course for you".

I had my reservations, but since Dr. Jones was on my Ph.D. committee that pretty much determined whether I received my Ph.D. degree or not, I gave in and agreed to retake the course. I absolutely knew at that moment; however, I had made a big mistake. I had my inside connections with a few of the graduate students who worked in the political science department and was told that I had been a topic of discussion with Dr. Plato, Dr. Jones, and other professors in the department. And it was not good.

During the semester, I would frequently go and visit with Dr. Jones to ensure I was always on the right track with my big project for their course. I never wanted it to come out that I had not followed directions, as I was preparing myself for a poor grade in the course. I just felt Dr. Jones was up to something, especially with his ties with Dr. Plato.

Dr. Jones always looked over my notes, data, and research paper, and always gave me the "thumbs up" approval. So, I proceeded with the project while even assisting some of the Carl Albert Fellows who were in the same course but struggling badly. These Fellows were considered some of the best and brightest political science graduate students, but here I was helping and tutoring them. The semester ended and I checked my grade to see that I made a C in Dr. Jones' course. I was upset, but not surprised at all. I immediately scheduled a meeting with Dr. Jones to voice my concerns.

I asked why I had received such a poor grade on my final research project despite having visited with him nearly every week to ensure I was on track with my project. We went over my data, the research project, and the paper highlighting how I had met the requirements for the project.

However, Dr. Jones still could not provide me with a definitive answer as to why I received the poor grade and was going to "stand behind" his decision. What infuriated me, even more, was the fact that some of the other students that I had assisted and tutored in the course which included some of the Fellows, all made A's. I worked my ass off in that class because I knew going into it that I had to as I already had a target on my back. I learned that no matter how hard I worked, it would not matter because of the arbitrariness and power that many of these professors had over my studies and my future.

But I was not going to let them win. I would do as I was told to do by my mentors, which was to pick and choose my battles and to jump through the necessary hoops. I needed to be strategic in the selection of my future courses for sure.

The spring 2006 semester was challenging due to Nikki's custody trial in February, but I had been on such a "high" being designated as the primary custodial parent for Nikki and being offered a full-time professor job at the community college.

But now that "high" quickly changed as I was having to mentally prepare for the upcoming semester at OU, as I found myself taking three courses (nine hours of graduate coursework) which is equivalent to attending full-time. I received A's in two of the courses – one of those courses being a required seminar course that was assumed to be one of the most challenging courses in the program – and a C in one of the other courses. What?! Here we go again! Guess who the professor was who assigned me my second C? Yep, it was Dr. Plato, the professor who was greatly offended that I had declined their offer to be their Graduate Assistant. A coincidence? I think not!

I immediately reached out to my mentors, who had been advising and mentoring me throughout the years and were crucial in preparing me for the challenges at OU. I told them what had happened in receiving my second C and that I had had enough and was going to withdraw from the Ph.D. program. I could see what the department was trying to do which I believed was to push me out of the program. Here I am now with two C's on my transcript for the program and receiving one more C, D, or F would mean being withdrawn from the program. I would rather withdraw on my own terms as opposed to letting that department kick me out.

I was so exhausted and defeated, but more upset than anything. I knew that I belonged in the Ph.D. program. I knew that I was just as smart as any of the graduate students in the Ph.D. program including many of the Fellows that I was assisting and tutoring who were receiving better grades than me in the same courses I was tutoring them in.

But they were part of the "clique" and here I was this non-traditional student that put my family and teaching responsibilities above my commitment to the political science department and boy was I going to continue to pay for that. But I was not going to let them win.

After several discussions with my mentors, I decided to remain focused and determined to push through the challenging political science department and its Ph.D. program at OU while being a full-time father and managing my teaching responsibilities.

The fall 2006 and spring 2007 semesters went pretty well but did have some challenges. As for my personal life, I was engaged to be married in March of 2007. However, my fiancé, Melissa, had a fragile relationship with her biological mother.

Melissa and I had met a few years prior when we both attended UCO. She was in one of my classes. Wait, let me clarify, as she was not one of my students. She and I were both students taking the same course. She was finishing up her undergraduate studies and I was finishing up my graduate studies. The course we were in was a mixed class with undergraduate and graduate students.

I had met Melissa's biological mother once. We met for lunch, and I thought it went extremely well, as we were all laughing and enjoying the conversations. Of course it went well, Melissa hadn't yet told her mother that we were dating. Once she did tell her, everything changed.

One day I could tell something was wrong with Melissa because she was acting differently. I had been around her long enough to know that something was wrong. I asked her and she divulged to me that her mother was not happy that we were dating and could not accept the fact that I was black. WHAT?! Here we go again. This is 2005-2006, people!

I had asked and received her father's permission to marry his daughter. Her mom, on the other hand, had been divorced from her dad and remarried for quite some time now.

You see, Melissa was white and her mom was this very traditional woman from Lahoma, a small town in Oklahoma, who firmly believed that Blacks and Whites should not "mix or marry", have relationships, or children. Was I upset? Absolutely. But not surprised based on my life experiences growing up with racism or prejudiced attitudes.

But the anger only lasted a few minutes. Melissa ended her relationship with her mother and chose me and Nikki. Melissa said that my daughter and I meant more to her than the ignorance of someone who happened to be family. Their relationship pretty much ended the day her mother made the decision not to support us and be a part of our family.

Additionally, I had endured racism for so long throughout my life that I was finally at a place that I was not going to let my mother-in-law's actions upset me or have any power over me. You see, the longer

I held on to this anger, the longer her mother had this power or control over my emotions and I was not going to let that happen. I allowed racist people for far too long to have power over me and I had learned to quickly move on. The way I looked at it was that it was her mother's loss.

I do not hate her mother by any means. The truth is, I feel sorry for her because she is the one who missed out over the years with the kids' birthdays, Thanksgiving, Christmas, graduations, etc. Her mother had these ingrained values and beliefs and was not going to back away from them. I know this may sound odd, but I respect her mother for staying true to herself and being honest with us even though I don't agree with her. But that's the thing; I do not have to agree with her and can move forward with my life with my family, and that is what I did.

As I was figuring out how to navigate the relationship with Melissa and her mom, I was also navigating my relationship with the chair of my committee at OU. They had become frustrated with me for wanting to complete equivalent courses at UCO.

This was part of my strategic maneuvering through the Ph.D. program: to take as many equivalent and transferable courses at other institutions to avoid certain professors who I believe had targeted me. This was not something uncommon, as my degree program allowed for a certain number of transferable courses from other institutions, so I was trying to maximize that option. I was strategizing.

Some of the other frustrations by my chair were simply miscommunication issues with the department secretary and not any fault of mine. I brought this to the attention of the chair in several emails. I always kept all emails through this department as documentation, as I believed I would need it one day.

The chair had also grown frustrated with me because he believed that I was not spending enough time on campus with the department and other graduate and Ph.D. students. I notified him in an email that I was simply stretched to capacity with teaching full-time and being a full-time father.

As I recall, his response was that I should quit my full-time job to be able to dedicate more time to the department. Seriously?! I was taken aback, as the majority of the Ph.D. students in the political science program with me were aspiring to be full-time professors, and here was my committee chair recommending that I give up my career...my ultimate dream job that I had been working so hard to obtain. Not gonna happen.

That exchange of emails and conversations over the next few months reiterated the fact for me that the department did not care about our teaching. What they wanted was for us to do their research for them, collect data, etc. But that was not what I wanted out of the program.

Several other Ph.D. students felt the same way. I was not the only non-traditional student who had been targeted. Nevertheless, I continued to jump through hoops and to be strategic in my decisions and selection of courses and professors.

I could still not get over the fact that this department could not recognize the importance of having non-traditional students in their program. There is a different perspective that we could bring to the program and share with the other students whether they were traditional or non-traditional.

The bottom line for me was that as long as I stayed on top of my studies, attended class, met with my professors and committee members – all of the formal things that should get me through this rigorous program – then I should not be targeted or pushed out of the program simply because I was not part of the "clique" or dedicated most of my life and time to the department.

Fall 2007 and spring 2008 semesters were GREAT semesters for me, as I was able to take courses outside of the political science department and in the Human Relations and Sociology departments, as those courses would complement my dissertation topic surrounding the death penalty. I loved these courses and the professors who taught them and they loved me as well.

Dr. Dorscine Spigner-Littles (Human Relations department) and Dr. Susan Sharp (Sociology department) were two other influential professors that would become extremely important mentors for me. There was such a different contrast between the two of them when compared to some of the dreadful professors that I endured in the political science department. Dr. Spigner-Littles and Dr. Sharp were not only well-known scholars within their fields, but they were sincere, humble, and cared for the success of their students. You truly felt that in their courses.

Each of them learned of my upbringing and struggles. They respected the fact that I was here at OU taking their courses in pursuit of a Ph.D. They embraced my non-traditional standing along with my life and work experiences that would greatly enhance class discussions.

Despite not taking any courses in the political science department during these past two semesters, I was still having to meet with my committee members to get signatures for course substitutions, course approvals, etc. It can be overwhelming. But I continued to push through.

I was getting excited as I was close to completing all of the required coursework to allow me to move on to the next stage of the Ph.D. process which was to take the general exams. At the pace I was going, I should have been ready to take my general exams about a year or so later, which would be the fall 2009 semester. But that did not happen and the political science department made sure of that.

I had pretty much completed all of my courses for the Ph.D. by the end of the spring 2009 semester, and that included 3 of the extremely rigorous "seminar" courses – one from each field of political science that I would be specializing in. I was proud of myself because I made As in all of them.

The goal was to take the entire summer to study and prepare for the general exams. General exams are brutal. You are locked in a classroom for eight hours and provided one unknown question for each of the three specializations you have selected as part of your degree. My three specializations were public policy, public administration, and American government. The expectation is that you answer each question by providing 20-30 scholarly sources and substance from articles, journals, books, etc. that you have covered throughout your academic studies. You are repeating everything that you have learned in regards to that specialization. You are provided a lengthy book list for each specialization to study and prepare, but you are not provided any notes, books, or articles, during the general exam. You are essentially having to regurgitate everything from memory within this eight-hour window. You are allowed small breaks to go to the restroom, but that's it. As for lunch, you are allowed to bring a lunch, snacks, or drinks, but are not allowed to leave the room for any length of time or to eat lunch. Once again, you are allowed to leave long enough to go to the restroom and that's it.

A few weeks before the end of my spring 2009 semester which was also my final semester of coursework, I reached out to the department secretary to ensure all of my paperwork had been signed off and approved, as I was trying to schedule general exams for the upcoming fall 2009 semester.

The department secretary called me and told me that we had a problem and that I was being withdrawn from the program. *What?!* Here we go again. I will be honest and say that I was extremely angry, but not surprised. I asked her why I was being withdrawn. She stated it was because I was simultaneously enrolled in two graduate programs: a Master's degree in Criminal Justice at UCO and the Ph.D. program at OU. I thought to myself: SO WHAT!! What's the big deal?

I firmly believed that the political science department was looking for any reason to have me withdrawn from their program, especially since I was able to strategically navigate through their program and complete all of my coursework without having received that final and fatal third grade of a C, D, or F which would have automatically had me withdrawn from the program. But I beat them and here I was finishing up my final semester of coursework.

I quickly explained to the department secretary that I had applied to the Master's degree in Criminal Justice at UCO back in the Summer of 2004 when I also applied for the Ph.D. in political science program at OU. I applied at UCO as a backup plan in case I was not accepted into the Ph.D. program. Though I was accepted into both programs, I never took any courses at UCO toward that Master's degree.

The department secretary stated that I could not be enrolled in two different graduate programs at the same time. Really?! I asked her if there was anything that could be done to resolve this issue as I was scheduled to take general exams this upcoming August which was only 4 months away. She said she would have to discuss it with the chair of the department, I believe, and get back to me. I WAS PISSED!!

My goal had been to use the entire summer to prepare for the general exams. We are now in May. A month had passed since I last spoke to the department secretary and I had still not received any word as to the status of the situation or what the resolution would be.

Despite summer soon approaching, I had not started to prepare for the general exams, as I did not know the status as to whether I would be able to take the general exams in August or even remain in the program. There was no way I was going to put myself and my family through my rigorous preparations for the general exams to only find out that I would be withdrawn from the program. So, I tried to contact the department secretary again, as I had done several times over the past few weeks and still no answer or resolution.

It was now June and still no word. I finally received a phone call from the department secretary with the news. I needed to have UCO withdraw me from their program. I got off the phone with the department secretary and immediately contacted the Graduate College at UCO and spoke to one of the advisors to explain my circumstances at OU. I was told since I was in "good standing" that UCO could not withdraw me from the program even with my request. This was UNBELIEVABLE. I told the advisor and now the dean that I was in good standing because I had not taken any courses despite being accepted into the program 5 years ago back in 2004. Nevertheless, I was told they could not withdraw me. RIDICULOUS!

I contacted the department secretary at OU and discussed with her that UCO could not withdraw me from their program. I asked her what can I do now? She said that perhaps I could get a "special exception" but it would have to be approved by the department chair. She said she would explain my circumstances with the department chair and get back to me.

A few weeks passed and it was now in July. Still no word from the department chair regarding my approval. I reached back out to the secretary in mid-July and still nothing. A few more weeks passed and we were now in the first week of August.

The summer passed and so did my opportunity to prepare and study for the general exams. I wasn't even sure if I would be taking any exams or remaining in the program at this point. I was frustrated and very upset.

Because I am someone that always prepares for the worst, I decided to take a couple of courses in the Ph.D. program in the Jeannine Rainbolt College of Education at OU during the summer while I was still waiting for a response from the department chair in the political science department regarding my special exception. I spoke to one of the main professors in the Ph.D. Educational Leadership and Policy Studies (ELPS) program, Dr. Courtney Vaughn, who learned of my circumstances with the political science department and she was not surprised. She welcomed me with open arms into their program if I chose to do so. She would go on to become one of my dearest mentors and friends.

The fall semester was just two weeks away from starting and I still had not heard anything regarding the department chair's approval to allow me to stay in the political science program despite being enrolled in another graduate program at UCO. I reached out to the department secretary for any updates. At this point, I was not even concerned about general exams anymore, as I believed I could reschedule them for the following spring 2010 semester. I was more concerned as to whether I could remain in the program.

The secretary responded, "I thought you knew. The department chair approved your special exception weeks ago to remain in our program despite you being concurrently enrolled in another graduate program."

I thought to myself, *HOW IN THE HELL WAS I SUPPOSED TO KNOW! I have learned a lot over my 38 years of life at this point, but reading minds was not one of them!* I set the phone down and placed my face into both of my hands trying not to scream.

She went on to say, "So you are all set to take your general exams this semester."

This was the final straw and I was done.

I felt the department and most of my committee members from the political science department were setting me up to fail. They were aware that I had not prepared for the general exams and now I was being told that I was clear to take the exams this semester. REALLY?! Preparing for general exams takes months.

I immediately reached out to Dr. Vaughn to discuss more about her program, my timeline for completing the Ph.D. in the ELPS program, transferring and applying graduate courses that I had already completed at UCO and OU, and, most importantly, applying for admission into their program.

Over the next few weeks, I met with several professors, advisors, and department chairs in the Ph.D. ELPS program and they were all extremely kind and excited for me to be a part of their "family." They were excited to have a student like me in their program that was very diverse; that is, a background in political science, criminal justice, sociology, and human relations, along with my teaching experience.

They looked at me as an asset with all that I had to bring to their program. They made me feel wanted and a part of their family, something that I had not felt since leaving UCO 5 years ago back in 2004. I had found my new home.

Once I was formally accepted into the Ph.D. in Educational Leadership and Policy Studies program, I sent a scolding email to the department secretary and all of the graduate and Ph.D. students in the political science department to notify them I was leaving the program and reiterated how I felt myself and other non-traditional students had been treated poorly. I went on to state how the department had a long-standing reputation of this behavior[14].

I had so many students and professors from OU reach out to me in a show of support and gratitude, as the words expressed in my email resonated with so many of them and it needed to be said.

The main purpose of my email, however, was like therapy for me. In other words, it was me lashing out like an abused victim, as I felt I had been abused by the department and their system for years and finally overcame my abuser by voicing through my email that they did not break me, so to speak. And I believe my actions will resonate with others as well reading this memoir, whether it's in academia, or in the professional, business sector, or any setting for that matter.

I was also told by several of the graduate and Ph.D. students that there was serious discussion amongst the faculty in the political science department after my email had been distributed and circulated throughout the department and the college. Even if no changes were going to be made within the department and how they treat non-traditional or any student for that matter, at least they were talking about it. But I was told that no significant changes were made. Not surprising, as arrogance shuts out humility.

The irony for me out of all of this with the department was that just a few years later I would be the department chair of the political science program at Oklahoma City Community College and wielded the hiring power for new adjunct (part-time) professors. Several OU students from the political science program would often contact me requesting a job. *#Karma.*

---

[14] See Appendix #1

The fall 2009 semester was very different than what I had experienced over the past four years with the political science department at OU. I was now a Ph.D. student in the ELPS program and I loved it! Most of my new committee members were extremely supportive, especially Dr. Courtney Vaughn, Dr. Dorscine Spigner-Littles, and Dr. Susan Sharp – I often refer to them as the "Big 3".

However, what I loved about my new program and path was that it allowed me to bring other disciplines: human relations, sociology, and political science into my research and dissertation topic that was still related to the death penalty. Had I been aware of the ELPS program before applying to the Ph.D. program in political science, I definitely would have gone the ELPS path and saved myself a lot of stress. I was not going to let the political science department derail my goal and dreams. I have always been a fighter. I strategized, persevered, and found another path. A better path. And here I was now in a supportive program.

Something else I loved about the ELPS program was how they worked extremely hard with me to apply as many of the graduate courses that I had previously completed within my political science degrees. Despite being approved to take my general exams with the political science department this fall 2009 semester, the change of programs pushed my new general exams back about a year or so. But this meant that I had to work extremely hard over the next year or so, going full-time and taking nine hours of graduate coursework each semester, including summers, while also managing my life.

The coursework and research alone with my studies were brutal and extremely time-consuming, but I knew that I needed to get through this while managing my other life commitments, as I was so close to obtaining the Ph.D. – a goal that I wanted to achieve, as it's the highest academic degree you could earn. But I was not only doing this for me. This Ph.D. was so much for my mother as well.

I did not necessarily need the Ph.D. now, as I was teaching full-time as a professor at OCCC which is where I felt the most comfortable and where I believed I had the most impact as opposed to teaching full-time at another institution, especially at a university.

I often thought of teaching full-time as a professor at a university, especially at UCO, but I truly felt that my life experiences would resonate more and have more of an impact with students at OCCC. The majority of community college students had a similar upbringing as me; growing up poor, gangs, raising children, having to work full-time, etc. while also trying to manage their academic studies.

We often hear of 'privilege'. Often, what that means, is a person has not had to face much in the way of societal adversity. They haven't had to prove themselves beyond merit. They haven't had to apply and receive and live off of financial aid and grants to be able to attend college. However, what I have noticed is that many who attend community colleges have indeed faced great adversity in their lives. In that way, I knew I could relate. More importantly, I knew I could help and I had a burning desire to inspire those students to chase their dreams.

For me, when I am in that classroom at OCCC, I can look at all of those students and tell them that I was once an OCCC student and sat in the very seats that they are sitting in right now. I can look at many of them who are struggling with life right now and share a little bit of my story with them. This resonates with them and, for many, inspires and motivates them because we can relate to each other. And if I was able to persevere through adversity and be where I am today as their professor, then they can achieve anything as well regardless of their circumstances.

And here I was pursuing a Ph.D. to fulfill my goal of achieving one, as I believed it may open even more doors for me. So, I stayed the course. Let's do this!

The fall 2009 and spring 2010 semesters were some of the best experiences I had as a Ph.D. student. I was taking education, sociology, and human relations courses and felt this is where I needed to be by being immersed in these disciplines. I learned that I was a sociologist at heart, as I loved the courses, discussions, and interactions with the other graduate students.

A lot of the research that I had done over the years in regards to public policy as it relates to the death penalty was sociologically based. I was often looking at the direct and societal effects of the death penalty. This is sociology, as it is the study of social life and behavior.

Though I had a few challenges with a couple of my ELPS committee members during these semesters, the "Big 3" kept things in order.

A year or so passed since being admitted into the Educational Leadership and Policy Studies Ph.D. program. I had completed 33 hours of required coursework for the new program, so you can say that I had been a little busy. I was killing myself to get through this coursework and I could not have gotten through this without the support from family, friends, and mentors.

It was now June of 2010 and I was preparing to take my general exams by the end of July. I had already been preparing for the past few months but was feeling good over the next few weeks leading up to the general exams. I was still very nervous though.

It's D-Day!! Tuesday, July 27th, 2010. General exam day. I had been waiting for this day for about 5 years. It was finally here, and I was prepared. As I was driving to the OU campus, I was reflecting on all of the 25-30 books and stacks of articles, studies, and research that I had examined over the years, but especially over the past few months in preparation for this day.

I arrived at 8:45 a.m. and walked into the office where the department secretary and assistant would guide me to the exam classroom. The assistant handed me the laptop that I was to use for the next eight hours.

Once inside the empty and stark room, I took my seat with the only items that were approved for me to have in my possession which was two sheets of paper with notes. That's it! I was expected to "dump" everything that I had ever read, learned, researched as it related to answering the two questions per the general exam.

I was typing, and typing, and typing, and by the time I looked up, it was already 1:00 p.m. I took a brief 10-15 minute break to eat the food and snacks that other professors and Ph.D. students had provided for me. Now that's how a family takes care of one another and the fact that other professors and Ph.D. students had brought me food and snacks only reassured me that I had made the right decision in joining the Educational Leadership and Policy Studies family.

After my brief break for food and snacks, I delved back into my general exams. I was pounding away at the keyboard trying to get as much information on paper as possible. I looked up and it was 4:30. I typed about 40 pages. I was mentally exhausted and couldn't write or cite anything more. Stick a fork in me, I am done!

My mentor, Dr. Brett Sharp at UCO said it perfectly regarding general exams in that, "when you are typing up your responses for the general exams in that 7 to 8-hour window, it will be during this time that you will be the smartest you have ever been in your entire life". And boy was he right! It was a grueling process, but I did it. Pass or fail, I did it. It was in the committee's hands now.

A couple of weeks later, I was now seated before my committee for the oral defense of my responses for the general exams. Not only do you have to answer the general exam questions on paper, but after you submit your responses, you have to orally defend them as well. And it is during this oral defense where you learn whether you have passed or failed. If you pass, you are no longer considered a Ph.D. "student" anymore. You are now a Ph.D. "candidate" and move on to the final step of the degree which is the dissertation. If you fail, you are done with the program and your academic journey and may be lucky to at least receive a Master's degree as a default, but no Ph.D. So, no pressure...

I went into the oral defense thinking it was going to be two hours of torture with committee members challenging everything that you had written for your responses. I heard horror stories regarding the oral defense, but my only reference was stories that I heard from the political science Ph.D. students. Boy was I wrong.

My oral defense was fun. I was able to effectively respond to all questions that were asked by all of my committee members. We shared some good discussions and laughs as well. What I learned from this committee and this program was that the oral defense was simply a formality. I pretty much passed when I completed the written phase of the general exams weeks ago. I believe my committee would not have allowed me to sit for the written part of the general exams if they truly believed that I was not fully prepared. The oral defense was simply my way to further show my committee that I was ready for the next step in my journey: the dissertation. I had passed my oral defense and was now a Ph.D. candidate and ABD. Hell yea!

Those three letters are what most Ph.D. candidates strive for. ABD stands for "All But Dissertation". This is a huge accomplishment, as it says that you are done with coursework and have passed your written and oral general exams.

Now the fun part begins, and I truly mean that, as the dissertation is writing a book based on your topic of interest supported by whatever methodology and data you wanted to collect and use to provide your rationale and conclusions. I was looking forward to this final journey for the Ph.D., but it would come with some challenges.

It was the fall 2010 semester, and I was working on my dissertation. I was religiously working on my dissertation all day every day. I know I was driving my committee chair, Dr. Vaughn, crazy, as I was speaking to her daily and emailing her drafts of my dissertation that revolved around the shared and lived experiences of those that had been directly or indirectly affected by murder and the death penalty.

The death penalty was a topic that I had been researching and writing on for the past 10 years at this time. I was first interested in the death penalty after my uncle was shot and killed in 1999. I submitted several research papers over the past 10 years while working on my Associate's, Bachelor's, and Master's degrees. My Master's thesis at

UCO, which I had to orally defend based on the death penalty, completed my final requirement for that degree back in 2004. I had also been collecting data in regards to the death penalty for years and even submitted some of my other research papers in some of my courses when I was pursuing my Ph.D. in the political science program just a few years ago. By the fall 2010 semester, I had an abundance of research, data, books, and articles which I believe gave me a significant jump or head start when finally beginning to work on my dissertation.

But despite my knowledge and expertise within the death penalty, there were a couple of my committee faculty members, whose knowledge was outside the scope of the death penalty and they began to make things extremely difficult for me when submitting drafts to the committee.

These two committee members, I'll refer to them as Dr. Bonnie and Dr. Clyde, were not well versed in policy as it relates to the death penalty which would be one of the main themes in my dissertation. They often provided negative feedback that they had "serious issues and concerns with the progress of this draft". All because the death penalty was something foreign to each of them.

However, my "Big 3" – that is, Dr. Vaughn, Dr. Dorscine Spigner-Littles, and Dr. Susan Sharp were all very experienced and knowledgeable regarding the death penalty as each of them had written and published articles and books surrounding the death penalty and the effects it had on society and its citizens.

They were all well-known, national researchers and scholars who held very prestigious and distinguished professorships at OU, and I was extremely blessed to have the "Big 3" on my committee. Plus, I knew having them on my committee would only enhance the quality of my research and work, as they were not going to sign off on a mediocre dissertation. They would only accept the very best work that met their extremely high expectations and that was another reason why I specifically selected them. I wanted the challenge. I wanted them to push me to be at my best.

The "Big 3" held things together despite the challenges and difficulties presented by Dr. Bonnie and Dr. Clyde. Don't get me wrong, I completely understand the concerns and issues that they had with the death penalty due to their lack of knowledge, but instead of providing all of the negative reviews of my drafts, the "Big 3" and I believed they could have handled things better.

I mean, my dissertation was not solely about the death penalty that fell within the disciplines of political science, sociology, and human relations. For my dissertation, I had to find a way to merge the death penalty with the Educational Studies literature and research. And I believe I did a great job in doing so with my initial drafts and the "Big 3" thought so as well.

After receiving a negative review by the other two committee members, I would have to schedule meetings with each of them to discuss and walk them through my drafts to provide better explanations and clarity and to show the connection I was making with the Educational Studies literature as well.

Dr. Clyde finally realized the difficulties he had been posing to me and the "Big 3" and decided that for the parts of my dissertation that dealt with more in-depth research regarding the death penalty that he would simply defer to the "Big 3" since they were all scholars in their own rights regarding the death penalty or at least interrelated topics and concepts surrounding the death penalty. However, Dr. Bonnie was not so easily persuaded and continued with her difficulties.

Dr. Bonnie continued to provide negative reviews with major revisions regarding my initial drafts despite the "Big 3" and Dr. Clyde now, who was providing minor edits and changes. Dr. Bonnie was causing a rift within the committee, as it just wasn't me who was growing more and more frustrated with her actions.

There was one particular committee meeting scheduled to discuss my dissertation progress and Dr. Bonnie did not show up. UGH! Please note, it's always extremely difficult to attempt to schedule a committee meeting with 5 committee members and myself based on our schedules.

At times, there would be several exchanges of phone calls and emails in an attempt to schedule a committee meeting that fit everyone's schedule. So, it was easy to understand everyone's frustrations when Dr. Bonnie failed to attend. And because she was not in attendance, the committee meeting had to be rescheduled.

I recall another committee meeting when my mentor and committee chair, Dr. Vaughn, had to kindly put Dr. Bonnie in her place and highlighted her disruptive actions that were not only upsetting the other committee members but were hindering my progress with the dissertation. She always fought so hard for me.

Dr. Vaughn was not having any more of this nonsense and neither were Dr. Littles and Dr. Sharp who were equally supportive and diligently fighting for me just as hard as Dr. Vaughn. And it helped that Dr. Sharp was my "outside committee member" as she wielded a lot of power and influence in protecting me and protecting me is what she did.

Shortly after this meeting, there were discussions to remove Dr. Bonnie from the committee and have her replaced. Perhaps the "Big 3's" stance and the talks that were spreading throughout the ELPS department that Dr. Bonnie may be replaced triggered something because Dr. Bonnie finally got on board with the committee. Now that everyone was on board, it made the next few months so much easier.

It was now the spring 2011 semester, and I was extremely close to getting through the remainder of my dissertation drafts and committee approvals, while also trudging through the extremely tedious process of getting what seemed like a million forms that I had to get signatures for from my committee, department secretary, department assistant, the dean, the department chair, the Institutional Review Board (IRB), and the graduate college. But this is the normal process. And despite my complaining about the process back then, I would not trade it for anything in the world because I was close to obtaining my Ph.D. My dissertation and presentation had been scheduled for Thursday, July 14th, 2011. I will never forget this date as not only would I be presenting and defending my dissertation this day, but it was also my birthday and I would be turning the big 40!

Over the next few weeks leading up to my dissertation defense and presentation, I was finalizing my drafts of each chapter of the dissertation and reflecting on those five participants who I had interviewed. Each of them had experienced a family member who had been either murdered, murdered someone, or had been executed and they were sharing these experiences with me.

Two of the interviewees were people I knew personally. One was my father who shared his story of losing his brother to "gang violence." Recall this was my uncle who was shot in the neck at the convenience store and bled to death. The other participant was Moe, who had lost his cousin who had been shot multiple times while backing his car out of a driveway after picking up a friend.

My dissertation was not only about conducting scholarly research and collecting data, but it was also extremely personal to me, as my uncle and cousin's death still bothered me at the time despite their murders some 10 years ago back in 1999. And it still bothers me to this day. I was hoping that my research could speak for them since they were not here to speak for themselves.

I was also hoping that my research would shed light on how murder and the death penalty affect so many people and families. Whether they were the victim or the offender (murderer), family's lives will forever be changed, and that is what I wanted to convey in my dissertation titled, "Impacts of Homicide and Death Penalty Experiences: A Hermeneutic Phenomenological Approach". Please see the abstract to shed some little light on my dissertation[15].

Not bad, huh, especially from someone who had come so far in their life. Just think, it was not too long ago that I was back in the 'hood, running the streets, dodging bullets, drinking, partying, etc. And now here I was preparing for my dissertation presentation and defense.

---

[15] See Appendix #2

Perhaps many candidates would have been nervous, but not me. I lived for being in front of an audience and presenting information, as, by this time in 2011, I had already been teaching as a professor for the past 8 years. The classroom was my sanctuary. It was my place of comfort and peace. I was ready to rock this presentation.

Melissa and I arrived at the conference room and were greeted by my committee chair, Dr. Vaughn. She pulled me aside and gave me a great big hug and kiss on the cheek and told me that she was very proud of me. Not only in terms of persevering through all of the adversity in striving for a Ph.D., but more importantly how far I had come in my life. She had always been extremely supportive of me and was fully aware of my life story. We just stood there and embraced one another and cried a little bit. Definitely tears of joy.

She released her bearhug on me and then told me to wait here in the hallway with Melissa until she came back out of the conference room.

After what seemed like an eternity, Dr. Vaughn came to get me. Just before going into the conference room, she looked at me and said, "Go get 'em, Tiger!" This was it! Melissa gave me a kiss and wished me good luck as she remained seated in the hallway.

My presentation and oral defense lasted about 2 hours and I believed went very well. I answered all of the questions from my committee members and was feeling good, but the committee had to vote unanimously and I was still concerned with two of my committee members. It was out of my hands at this point. I did the best I could and left it all in that conference room.

Dr. Vaughn then mentioned that the committee members needed to briefly deliberate and that I needed to exit the room. I waited in the hallway with Melissa who was very nervous. She and I were talking and I was snacking while constantly looking at my watch. 10 minutes passed. 20 minutes. At this moment, I was thinking about my mother. I knew she would still be proud of me even if I failed. I truly knew that. But I would still feel like I disappointed her despite all of the academic achievements since going back to college back in 1999.

As I stood there reflecting on my academic journey, Dr. Vaughn opened the conference door. "Congratulations, DR. SMITH!" Oh. My. God. I was speechless. Everything around me went silent. Melissa was hugging me. Dr. Vaughn was hugging me and they were both saying something, but I had no idea what they were saying because it was like I had gone deaf. I felt I was in a dream or something. I was still in awe.

"Dr. Smith, please come join the committee," said Dr. Vaughn, as she was walking back into the conference room. I knew this was not a dream. As I walked into the conference room, the committee members were standing and clapping. They all came and gave me hugs and congratulations. We talked for a few minutes about publishing my research. They believed that it was worthy of publication!

As we adjourned from the classroom, I made 4 phone calls as I am walking to my car. The first was to my mother to notify her that her son had passed and was now "Dr. Smith." She was so overwhelmed with joy that she broke down and began to cry. She was so very proud[16].

The remaining phone calls I made were to my mentors, Dr. Scott, Dr. Sharp, and Professor Glencross who had been so instrumental in this journey with me. I can say with certainty had they not been there for me throughout this 7-year Ph.D. journey, I would have quit a long time ago. But it was them who continued to encourage me to push through the adversity I had been subjected to in my initial pursuit of the Ph.D. I was now Dr. Smith and it felt really good[17].

Please see all of the academic awards and recognitions that I received on my journey to the Ph.D. hood and beyond[18]. I share these not to brag, boast, or otherwise elevate myself. I share these to show how far a kid from the 'hood had come.

I also hope these awards and recognitions serve to inspire and motivate others to show what hard work, dedication, perseverance, and discipline can do for you. If I can get myself out of the 'hood and into

---

[16] See photo #14
[17] See photo #15
[18] See Appendix #3

the Ph.D. hood, so can you! Don't let anyone convince you that you *must* become a product of your environment. Don't allow yourself to become convinced that you're somehow stuck. Don't believe you are being disloyal by getting out and taking care of yourself. Quite the contrary! By being and becoming the best version of you, it will allow you to remain loyal and to give back to those who have always been there for you.

PART THREE

SERVING THE 'HOOD

CHAPTER ONE

SEMINARY, HARVARD, AND WHAT MAY HAVE BEEN

It was the summer of 2011 and I had just successfully defended my research and data as the final step in obtaining my Ph.D. I was finally done with my academic journey, correct? NOPE!

You would think with all that I had achieved at this point in my life regarding academics that I would be satisfied. But those who know me know that I am just wired a little differently. I am never one to be satisfied, which is often a blessing and a curse.

Without skipping a beat, I applied and was accepted into the Certificate of Graduate Theological Studies (CGTS) program at Phillips Theological Seminary in Tulsa, Oklahoma, and would begin taking classes in the fall of 2011. I was impressed with what each of my professors brought to Phillips, as they were all well-respected within the theological community with backgrounds from Harvard, Princeton,

Notre Dame, Vanderbilt, and other prestigious colleges and universities known for their theology, divinity, and religious studies.

You are probably wondering why I wanted to go to seminary. Well, I can tell you that it was not to seek work or a career in the ministry or church by any means. I attended seminary purely for the knowledge and was extremely excited to take my first course. I do have to thank my dear friend, Shannon, who encouraged me to attend Phillips, as she believed that my background and expertise in political science and public policy would benefit the education environment at Philips and I would benefit from them as well. I was told I would be "groundbreaking" by one of the board members, Kyle, who would become one of my biggest supporters and friends.

I also have to thank my former pastor, "Ms. Debi" and her amazing husband, Kyle, and First Christian Church in Yukon, Oklahoma for providing a scholarship that afforded me the opportunity to attend seminary. Seminary ain't cheap!

I was heavily recruited, and it was an easy decision. Theology had always been a subject of interest to me. I mean, living in the Bible Belt, you cannot help but be immersed in religion. You constantly see religion impact and affect public policy and laws, and there's literally a church on every corner in Oklahoma. As I had done with my Ph.D. studies, I was merging all of my specializations with theology. My main goal was to thoroughly examine how religion affects public policy and voting behavior.

My other goal in attending seminary was to aid in my plans to create and teach a Religion and Politics in America course at the colleges where I was currently teaching. I also wanted the knowledge and information to educate and inform my students and others, as religion has often been used as a tool to marginalize and exclude certain groups of people for thousands of years.

Religion often casts a veil of ignorance over people and to combat ignorance, you need to educate, as ignorance is simply the lack of knowledge. One of my favorite classical philosophers, Socrates, said it nicely when he said, "There is only one good, knowledge; and only one evil, ignorance." I could not wait to attend Phillips.

I received a lot of attention while on campus as many students and faculty were fascinated with my academic background. Here I was with all of this knowledge in political science, public policy, sociology, human relations, and education and was seeking a certificate in theology with no aspirations of working in the ministry or church. This made my presence on campus intriguing to many. And I was honored that so many people were interested in my academic background and journey.

I immersed myself in a well-rounded program of study but focused mainly on the history of Christianity. My absolute favorite course, however, was "Introduction to the Hebrew Bible". Though I enjoyed all of my courses, the Bible courses were the ones I enjoyed the most. I enjoyed those courses because there are so many public policies and laws that are and have been extremely influenced by interpretations of the Bible. I wanted to dissect every single chapter and scripture in the Bible. And I did!

I was blown away and despite the rigors of this course, I was completely fascinated with the hundreds of different interpretations of the Bible as provided by hundreds of theological scholars from all over the world that provided their perspectives in our study Bible for the course. I learned that what the Bible says and what the Bible *actually* says are two entirely different things.

I loved my year and a half journey and experiences at Phillips. It was challenging, but I knew what I was getting myself into and wanted the academic challenge. All of my professors challenged each of us to be open-minded, think critically, and understand that there are things in the Bible that are historic, metaphors, and subjective and cannot be taken literally in all aspects. Wow!!

I was absolutely not expecting professors at a seminary to challenge us to think critically and to be open-minded. My perception was that seminaries indoctrinated you; to shove all of this information regarding the Bible down your throats and force you to accept it all as the truth without question. That was one of my biggest hesitations in considering attending a seminary. But I was ignorant to think that way and I enjoyed this enlightenment provided by Phillips.

By spring 2013, I graduated with my CGTS. I was extremely proud of myself as I graduated with a 3.90 GPA. I had a great time at Phillips. No drama. Great education.

With my certificate behind me, I was finally done with my academic journey, correct? NOPE! Immediately after completing my studies at Phillips, I traveled to Harvard University to complete a leadership course, as I was building up my resume for possible leadership and administration positions in higher education.

It's the summer of 2013 in Cambridge, Massachusetts, and I will never forget walking on to the campus of Harvard University. Despite it being summer, I was definitely surprised by the cool and dry brisk breeze that touched my face. I was so used to the extremely hot and humid summers back in Oklahoma, but it was very different here in Cambridge, and I loved it! As I am walking across the campus checking out all of the wonderful sights, I definitely began to wonder how my life may have turned out had I accepted the offer years ago from Dr. Scott, Dr. Sharp and the dean at UCO to attend Harvard or any Ivy League school.

As I am walking across campus and taking it all in, I stop dead in my tracks and think, "Wow, I am walking across the campus of Harvard." It really hit me hard that here I am, some guy from the 'hood with a troubled past is now on the campus of this very prestigious university. I mean, I had always dreamed of attending and walking on the campus at Harvard and often seen its images on television and others being accepted and attending, but I never dreamed in a million years of this moment, as I am standing in complete awe. I would go on to complete my leadership course and truly enjoyed my stay and time at Harvard University.

I enjoyed it so much that a few weeks later, I began taking Massive Open Online Courses (MOOC) at Harvard University – or, their HarvardX free online courses. And despite the perception that online courses may be a lot easier than on-campus courses, especially since these online courses were free, they were all extremely rigorous and challenging. There were a lot of required readings, watching video lectures, and exams. And in order to receive an actual HarvardX Certificate, you had to meet a minimum overall score on all of your quizzes and exams.

I completed several courses and received the certificates for each as I wanted the challenge in completing the courses as opposed to simply having access to the information for informational purposes. My thoughts were that if I was going to spending several hours a week reading, viewing lectures, completing quizzes and exams, then I should do what it took to receive an actual certificate. That was just the drive that I had and always had.

CHAPTER TWO

THE ROAD TO REAL ESTATE

By January of 2015, I decided to enroll in real estate school to get my license. Over the years, people have asked me why I chose to get into real estate. It's not a simple explanation, so let me provide the full background and context, as the main reason for getting into real estate will anger you. And it should.

It was the summer of 2010 and Melissa and I were ready to downsize our home since Nikki, being an adult now, would be moving out soon to attend college. We would be going from a family of four to a family of 3 and just no longer required as much space. Nikki had also decided to move back to Colorado the next summer to be able to spend time with her half-brother and sister as they were entering important stages in their lives and headed to middle school and high school. We discussed it and I thought it was a great idea. Nikki was almost nineteen and I firmly believed that her time with me raising her since she was twelve years old was the most crucial in terms of teaching her the discipline, values, beliefs, morals, ethics, and other qualities she needed to be a good human being. I knew that I had instilled these values in her when she was a lot younger as well, but I believed these adolescent years were the most important. I was, and still am, grateful that I was able to give her these gifts which I believed to be the ideal characteristics and values that would follow her for the rest of her life.

In the summer of 2010, in preparation for Nikki being gone the following year, leaving just Melissa, our son Dylan, and myself, we decided to put our home up for sale. Dylan was ten years old and I had raised him since he was five years old because his biological father had been absent over the years. He was my son.

Our current home needed to be sold, so I reached out to a dear friend of mine who had been a licensed real estate agent for years but was only doing it part-time. However, he was a friend, and of course, I sought his assistance first. He had assisted me in purchasing my first home just a few years earlier in 2005 and told me he would give me a huge discount. I definitely could not pass on a discount. He listed our home in July of 2010 and it sat for nearly 3 months without any offers. It was now late October and winter was approaching, so we decided to take the home off the market. I was definitely disappointed.

The following spring of 2011, I reached out to another dear friend of mine who was also a part-time real estate agent. He offered a discount as well and was aware of the situation the previous year when we could not get the home sold. He listed the home for sale, and it sat on the market for nearly 6 months. It was now late October and no offers, so we decided to take the home off the market again.

Melissa and I were frustrated, to say the least. By this time, Nikki was already back in Colorado and it was just the three of us in a home too large for us. We just did not need all of that space. Based on our previous unsuccessful experiences with trying to sell the home, we did not try to list our home for sale again until March of 2014. And when Melissa and I discussed listing it for sale again, she stated, "Babe, I know both of your real estate agent friends provided us a discount to sell our home, for which I am extremely grateful, but I would rather us pay more money and use full-time real estate agents as opposed to part-time agents." I definitely agreed. I did not know who we would use, but the decision would be unexpectedly made for us.

Our sweet, elderly neighbors directly across the street from us were selling their home. About a week or so after their Keller Williams "FOR SALE" sign was placed in their yard; I came home to see a "SOLD" sign now in their yard. I knew right then that Melissa and I had found our real estate agent. I did not believe this to be a coincidence. We found him for a reason.

I reached out to this full-time, top-producing Keller Williams real estate agent and he had our home sold and closed in about 45 days. I was simply blown away when compared to the two previous attempts to sell the home. And this real estate agent would go on to become my mentor at Keller Williams.

Now we were off to move into my rental property – the first home I had ever purchased back in 2005. We moved back into that home to force me to do the necessary updates to sell the home, as I no longer wanted to be a landlord and deal with the upkeep, maintenance, and bad tenants over the years with the rental property. Moving into the rental property was certainly an adjustment. We had gone from a nearly 3000 square foot home to now a 1300 square foot home. But we knew that this stay would be short-lived, as we were building a brand-new home that would be ready in about 6 months. The updating and remodeling began on the investment property that we were now living in. And before we knew it, it was late October and we listed the home for sale with the same Keller Williams real estate agent that had sold our previous home.

Just 5 days later, the real estate agent had our home sold. Once again, I was blown away.

I vividly remember sitting in my home office with the real estate agent signing forms and telling him how impressed I was with his selling both of our homes. I remember asking him, "How do you sell homes so fast? How do you do it?" He responded with a great big smile and said, "Brother, you can do this as well! You have the personality and wits to do what I did. One of the most important things you need to have in real estate is a great network and based on your already large network of students, professors, administrators, family, and friends, you can do this! Your social network is as large if not larger than mine, so I know you would be great as a real estate agent." The seed was planted.

However, when people over the years ask me why I really got into real estate, it was due to the very toxic and punitive retaliatory culture that was so prevalent for years at Oklahoma City Community College. It was so bad and affected me and others, that I needed to find another means of income and job stability.

This was extremely sad for me, because I had felt the college had done so much for me as a former student and graduate, and I wanted to give back to the college by coming back and being a full-time professor. However, extremely bad supervisors and administration slowly took away that family feeling and love that I once had for the college. I was sad and extremely disappointed.

I was fearful that I would soon be forced out or fired by the college which was something that had happened to several faculty, staff, and employees throughout the years when you spoke out against or filed a grievance against a bad supervisor or administrator.

So, in January of 2015, I enrolled in a real estate school. Over the next few months, I immersed myself in all of the HGTV and Bravo TV shows that highlighted everything that had to do with real estate. I was absolutely hooked!

I would record several episodes and binge watch them over the weekend. When most people were out on Friday or Saturday nights partying and having fun, I was at home watching back-to-back episodes for hours, often times watching them while dressed up in a suit, as I had to be dressed for the part while viewing some of these top-producing, multi-million-dollar agents, right? Melissa thought I had lost my mind.

In addition, I would oftentimes envision myself meeting with clients, conducting open houses, negotiating deals for my clients, and so much more.

And by July, I was a licensed real estate agent. I was extremely excited about where this new endeavor would take me. There were some challenges in the beginning, but more importantly, I had another option that would provide the much-needed financial stability I so desperately needed due to the bad supervisors and administration that I believed had continued to target, harass, and penalize me.

CHAPTER THREE

ROUGH START, RACISM AND REAL ESTATE

I received my license in the middle of the year which placed me at a disadvantage, as I only had 6 months to impact lives and begin, according to my real estate motto: "Making Dreams a Reality" for my new buyers and sellers. I finished up 2015 as a real estate agent with only five closings. The average agent closes about 8-12 a year. Nevertheless, I was still disappointed in myself despite my shorter timeline, but as you know by now, I hold myself to extremely high expectations.

Though I would go on to be a top-producing real estate agent by the following year, there were some challenges and struggles that I endured that not too many other agents have experienced based on the color of their skin.

Here's the thing; I am not attempting to turn my memoir into something all about racism. I am not some angry black power militant who believes that all white people are racist. That would be just as ignorant as the racist and prejudiced people I have encountered throughout my life. Even so, the majority of my closest friends, family, and mentors are white.

I do believe it is important to share with you my experiences in dealing with the racism that I have endured my entire life and real estate just so happens to be one of those areas. You see, I am already at a disadvantage being a real estate agent of color, being biracial. According to national data, the average real estate agent is a 55-year-old white female who attended college and owned a home. And 64% of real estate agents are female. In addition, data provides that Black real estate agents comprise only 5%-6% of agents, sell the least expensive homes, and have the lowest median income on average.

There is a multitude of factors that can explain the extremely low representation of Black real estate agents. One of the factors is racism. Early in my career, and on more than one occasion, I had white clients who told me that their elderly parents were not comfortable working with a black real estate agent. I have also heard and seen the very negative stereotype that is commonly associated with black real estate agents or other agents of color. That is, we are lazy, uneducated, lack the social personality, and are simply not equipped to be effective real estate agents. I know some of you may be blown away by this, but it happens more often than you can imagine.

Please understand that there are a lot of potential real estate clients who simply judge you by the color of your skin. They have no idea that you may be a real estate agent that has two Master's degrees and a Ph.D. and taught as a college professor for nearly 20 years. They simply meet with you and before you can start your presentation with them, they look at you up and down, scanning you, and make a comment like, "Oh, I had expected something different. This is not going to work for us, sorry." And based on my experiences, I knew exactly what that meant.

My appearance is business professional attire, as I am always in a suit and tie. I have even had clients be bold enough to tell me, "Oh, we did not know you were black. This is *definitely* not going to work." At least I could respect them for being honest.

I would have to dedicate an entire book to all of the incidents where I've encountered prejudice and racism, but I can share this one quickly. It happened when I met an elderly white man and his granddaughter. It was February of 2016, and I was an exclusive listing agent for a reputable builder and had the opportunity to list and sell several homes for him. There was a brand new home in a good neighborhood and community in Oklahoma City. The grandfather, Fred, called me and asked if he could view a home as he wanted to purchase it for his granddaughter. I agreed to meet him at the home the following day. I arrived a few minutes early, which I always do, and went inside to turn on all of the lights and open up all of the blinds. As I was making my way to the front office of the home, I could see outside the window this elderly gentleman (probably in his 70s) and his granddaughter pull up next to the curb and parked in the street.

As I made my way out of the house to meet him in the driveway, I said, "Hello, you must be Fred." He replied, "Oh, you're a colored." To which I ignored and went on to introduce myself. Trust me, I was extremely angry, but did not let it show. I fought hard to suppress the 'hood rage and anger that wanted to tell John to get the hell out of my face with that BS, but I kept calm, composed, and professional.

He was a very cranky old man and just had a really poor attitude. I say poor attitude because before we could even make it inside the home, he was criticizing the builder and how the exterior of the home appeared. Fred had mentioned that he was once a builder himself and continued his criticisms along with his granddaughter who was probably in her early to mid-twenties. I simply explained that the exterior was a popular exterior for this area.

We continued making our way to the front door when he said, "Did some Arab build this home? You know these Arabs are buying up all this land and building these crappy homes!" *Guys, I cannot and I am NOT making this up.* To which I replied, "He is a reputable builder and he and his family have been building really great homes for well over 20 years."

Fred sort of grumbled to himself and finally he and his granddaughter made their way into the house where it only gets worse…much worse. John immediately makes his way to the kitchen and it's gorgeous with all stainless appliances, a large kitchen island with pendant lights, quartz countertops, a walk-in pantry, etc. But Fred's only concern was the plumbing as he opened the cabinets under the sink to view the plumbing lines.

I thought this was odd, but I continued my presentation of the home by bringing attention to all of the upgrades and amenities of the home. By this time, Fred was fully laying on the kitchen floor and literally in the cabinet under the kitchen sink yelling, "This is SHIT! This is the worst plumbing I have ever seen in my entire life!"

At this point, I was fed up and could not endure any more of his criticisms and poor attitude towards me. It was at that time that I said in a calm voice, "Fred, it's time for you and your granddaughter to leave now because it is obvious that you do not like this home." To which he replied, "I would not buy this piece of shit home! And you can tell your Arab builder that he doesn't have a clue on how to build a home." To which I replied, "Okay, Fred, but I just need you to leave now, please."

Apparently, my request to ask Fred to leave upset his granddaughter, as she got involved and said, "Don't talk to my grandfather like that!"

"It's apparent he does not like the house, and I am done listening to him yell and curse at me, so you need to leave, too, or I will call the police," I answered.

When the granddaughter heard "police" she quickly moved over to Fred and was escorting him toward the front door. She was behind him and had her hand on the small of Fred's back slightly guiding him to the front door. Fred was still yelling and cursing as he was slowly making his way to the front door but stopping every few feet or so to point out other items he was not happy with regarding the home. I asked him once again to just leave, as I was now behind the granddaughter.

It was then that the granddaughter turned to face me and yelled, "STOP TALKING TO MY GRANDFATHER LIKE THAT, YOU FUCKING NIGGER!" as she proceeded to spit in my face. *Yep, that just happened.* I will be honest and say that my natural reaction was to slap the mess out of her, but I refrained from doing so. It was one of the most difficult things that I had ever had to do in my life.

I am just being honest here. I had been called a "nigger" throughout my entire life so I was used to that. It's kind of crazy just thinking about it, that I had come to be used to that. But, I had never had anyone spit in my face before. Ever! I saw red, and that usually meant that I was going to whoop that ass! But something inside of me held it together. I believe I had the Poos family to thank for that because my years of martial arts at that time had taught me self-control and patience and not to immediately react in situations like this. And I knew better than to react the way I wanted to. I was better than that and I was better than them.

I wiped the spit from my face and said to the granddaughter, "You know that you just committed a felony, right? I am calling the police!" I am not sure about laws in other states, but in Oklahoma spitting on someone is considered a felony. The granddaughter's eyes immediately got big when she heard "felony" and "police" and was now pushing Fred to the front door. Once outside, she and Fred hurried to get in their car. I made my way to the back of the vehicle to take pictures of their car and tag number as I was calling the police at this time. They quickly drove off while I was reporting the incident to the police. I used a towel to wipe the remaining spit from my face and made my way back into the house to wash up.

I met with an Oklahoma City Police Detective a few days later to provide my statement and the towel as they said they would try to extract some DNA from it if they could. I also provided Fred's telephone number as well. The detective told me that he would follow up, but did not know what, if anything, would happen to Fred or the granddaughter as it would simply be my word against theirs. I knew they were most likely not going to spend the money to have a lab test my towel when compared to other cases that were more important than mine. Even if something were done, I would never know, as I believe the detective told me that he would not be contacting me for an update, so I just left it at that. I let it go.

In other words, I let the anger I had towards Fred and his granddaughter go because the longer I held on to that anger, the longer I would be giving them power over me and they were not worth that. I can assure you, however, had this occurred some 20 years prior (when in my 20s), I most likely would have retaliated and it would not have been good for Fred and his granddaughter, and I would most likely be writing this memoir from a jail or prison cell. #FACTS

But I truly believe my years of martial arts experience is what saved Fred and his granddaughter and saved me from myself, as the spirit and essence of taekwondo and the Poos family taught me self-control and patience during times like this.

That event definitely made me reconsider whether I was cut out to deal with people like Fred and his granddaughter as I was just beginning this new real estate journey. But I told myself that I would not let people like Fred and his granddaughter deter me from something that I truly enjoyed. And I really wanted real estate to work out due to my issues at the community college. So I put this event aside and moved on.

To this day, I still have Fred's phone number and text messages from 2016 when he was inquiring about the house before our meeting. I have him saved in my phone as *"Fred (asshole and GD spit in my face)"*. I have kept his number and text messages to remind me that I am better than people like that[19].

And even though he and his granddaughter had no respect for me, I was still able to be respectful to them despite them not deserving any kind of respect.

And every once in a while, I look at his number and text messages as it also serves as a reminder of my growth as a person.

---

[19] See photo #16

The harsh reality is that this was not the last time something like this happened to me and I know it will not be the last. Unfortunately, these are examples of what some black real estate agents (or any real estate agents of color) experience in their careers.

Could this be the reason why black representation amongst real estate agents is only 5%-6%? Could it be the reason why black agents typically sell the least expensive homes? Could this be the reason why black top-producing agents (closing about $2M a year) constitute a small group of real estate agents in general? The answer: It could be, yes.

However, I will not sit here and say that racism is the *sole* factor to explain why black representation among real estate agents is significantly low. I will be honest here, as that is the only way I know how to be, and say that some of it is our fault. I hate to say it but unfortunately, I have worked with black agents who fit the negative stereotype and make it extremely difficult for other black real estate agents.

For example, I have worked with several *experienced* black real estate agents over the years who are unorganized, unprofessional, show up to view homes with their clients in jeans and a t-shirt, lack of communication, multiple errors when sending paperwork, knowing there is a problem gaining access to their seller's home and not doing anything about it, not meeting specific time-sensitive deadlines per the contract, asking me to draft up the offer/contract for their clients, and so much more. And I have had discussions with other black agents who are also frustrated when working with other black agents that are not on top of their game, so to speak.

Please do not get me wrong. I completely understand if these issues were from a lack of training. I get that and often tell the agents that I am here to help them, and I have helped many of them throughout the entire process. But there are some things that you should not need training for, such as simply dressing professionally. Real estate is a professional business where there is an exchange of thousands and sometimes millions of dollars.

And I know that I will have offended some black real estate agents and just some real estate agents in general in regards to my attire remarks. Dressing professionally is my opinion and not meant to offend anyone. I know many real estate agents that have adopted more of a casual-style in terms of their attire and that's okay, as it may work for them and their clients. You do you!

But I am of the opinion that as real estate agents, we should dress professionally. And I do, whether I am meeting with a family member, friend, or client to buy or sell a $50,000 home or a million-dollar home. It's just my preference and we can respectfully agree to disagree.

And, at times, it has gotten me in trouble, as I was showing a gorgeous home a few years ago with some of my dear friends (Jeremy and Ashlee) in Blanchard, Oklahoma. The home was located in a pretty rural area on a couple of acres. As we were leaving the home and headed to the next one, I get into my car and immediately smell poop. I get out of my SUV, dressed in my usual suit and tie and rocking the matching Vans shoes, and saw that I had stepped in some poop. Jeremy and Ashlee were laughing hysterically and he made some comment like: "we definitely have to get this city boy back to the city." It was hilarious, and I am glad I had some paper towels and Windex in my real estate survival pack to clean off my Vans. Just a casualty of dressing professionally, I guess.

However, we have to do better as black real estate agents, and I am extremely pleased to see several real estate brokerages all over the nation identify the problems and implement initiatives and programs dedicated especially for the success of black real estate agents. And I am glad to be a part of these programs in that I can provide my knowledge and experiences and sort of act as a mentor, as I want all real estate agents to be as successful as I have been blessed to be.

CHAPTER FOUR

FIRST TASTE OF SUCCESS

It was not easy in the beginning of my real estate career, but nothing in my life came easy, and I was extremely focused on being the best real estate agent I could be. I pushed myself hard and it paid off in a very short time.

By the end of my first full year of real estate in 2016, I closed on twenty-three homes. That was a huge accomplishment for me, as the average agent closes eight to twelve a year. I was officially considered and labeled a "Top-Producer" having sold at least $2M in a single year. This year only fueled my desire and motivation to do even better the following year. I was being acknowledged throughout the real estate industry as a "rising star" and knew that I had been extremely blessed.

In 2017, I closed on thirty-seven homes. I was proud of myself, but I was even prouder that I had made dreams a reality for thirty-seven families. They were my motivation. I received several recognitions and awards again and was extremely grateful. My real estate business was growing, but I challenged myself to assist more families the following year despite still teaching full-time as a professor.

It was also in 2017 when I officially formed the Markus Smith Real Estate Team, LLC. I was a one-man "team" but I soon began to mentor and assist a couple of longtime friends, Alonzo Harris and Althea Hall, who would go on to get their real estate licenses. I also became a mentor and friend to a young and aspiring agent, Anthony, who left his former broker and came to join me at Keller Williams Realty Elite. He and I and his wife, Kailey, and their son, A.J., instantly bonded and we all became really close like family.

In 2018, I closed on forty-five homes. Growth! I loved this new career and assisting even more families than the previous year. Additional accolades and awards came my way, but more importantly, I had truly found my passion in real estate. By this time in my real estate career, I was now ranked in the top 5% of real estate agents in Oklahoma.

There are about 10,000 agents in the entire state and about 6,000 in the Oklahoma City Metro alone, so to be a part of that top 5%, I was honored and humbled. I was also climbing the ranks within my top-producing brokerage, as I was producing more as an individual agent than some of the teams in my office. But you guys know where I am going with this…. I challenged myself to do more the next year. It would be a good year, but with some hardships.

In 2019, I closed on sixty-one homes. I will never forget this year as it was this year when I sold my first million-dollar, luxury home. My commission check was $53,000.00[20]. This one check alone was more than my yearly base salary at the college, as I was still teaching full-time as a professor. And the only way that I was able to make real estate work while juggling my duties and responsibilities as a professor is due to my extremely flexible teaching schedule and the assistance of Alonzo, Althea and Michael, who had come on board that year as well.

---

[20] See photo #17

When I received that commission check, I was overwhelmed with joy. I walked out of the title company with my check in hand and headed straight to my car. I am walking particularly fast, as it is getting harder and harder for me to just walk as my knees are trying to buckle on me and I am trying not to fall and make a scene.

I finally reached my car and started crying profusely. I set the check on my dash and just stared at it for a few minutes while wiping the tears that continued to roll down my face. I do not know why this hit me so hard. I thought back on my life. I thought back when my mother and I were seated at the small dining table in our small kitchen in our small home in the 'hood and working on my math problems late at night. I thought about the exhaustion I saw in my mother's eyes, but also her gentle smile when I answered the question correctly.

Who would have thought that this kid from the 'hood would be sitting in his car holding this check for $53,000 which was the largest transaction and commission check that I had received at that time? I am still trying to figure out why it had this impact on me. Perhaps it was the fact that it was a million-dollar home in a very affluent neighborhood that was so far from the type of house and neighborhood that I had grown up in.

I had always heard about these homes when growing up but never thought in my wildest dreams that I would ever be able to purchase one but let alone be able to be trusted to sell one for my client. Perhaps it was the fact that I could remember helping my mother clean dirty, filthy, and nasty hotel rooms when I was younger and now here I was helping to stage and sell million-dollar homes. I do not know what it was about this transaction, but I will never forget that feeling.

2019 was also a great year for me, as I was acknowledged by my office at Keller Williams Realty Elite – which also happens to be one of the top-producing offices in Oklahoma. The office has over 200 agents, many of them are some of the top agents and teams in the state and nation, and I was presented with an award for closing the most individual units in 2019 (61 total). It was my best year yet, and a lot of work, but I was happy with the number of families I was able to assist. It's always about the families.

This was also the year that I ventured out and hired the best Transaction Coordinator in the business, Tracey Medrano. Tracey acted as a processor and took over all of the important administrative items such as getting signatures for forms and contracts, contacting clients, realtors, lenders, title companies. This freed up a lot of my time to grow the business even more and boy did it grow the following year. And I was also proud of some of my "team members" – Althea Hall, Alonzo Harris, and Michael Knight, who I had mentored and assisted as well in getting them and their clients to the closing table to close on their homes. I say "team members" but I do not have a traditional "team" as typically found in most real estate offices. With most traditional teams, all transactions go through the Team Leader and the sales and commissions are usually split between the Team Leader and the other real estate agents.

But my unconventional team consists of three part-time real estate agents that already have full-time, good paying jobs with benefits. They are doing real estate as a side hustle for the additional income. My role is more of a mentor and to assist them with their transactions when their full-time careers do not provide them the flexibility to meet their clients' needs and demands, but we always make it work for their clients.

We simply help each other and fill in when they may not be able to meet with their clients which is extremely rare, but it's good to know that I have their backs when needed and they have mine.

Though 2019 was my best year yet in terms of real estate, it was one of my worst years personally, due to my circumstances as a professor at OCCC; an institution I had taught at since 2004.

CHAPTER FIVE

ME VS. OCCC

Remember, the main reason I got into real estate was due to years of what I perceived as being subjected to a toxic culture of bad supervisors, administration, and an HR department that did not provide any relief for several faculty, staff, and employees who had filed grievances against bad supervisors and administrators.

The college had a history of a very retaliatory and punitive culture. I was simply one of many that fell victim to this culture and endured it for years. It took a significant toll on me physically, mentally, and spiritually, as well as my family. I lost weight. My hair was falling out. I developed migraine headaches. I was a mess but hid it well whether I was in the classroom with my amazing students or with clients when meeting with them for a listing presentation or showing homes.

However, in 2019, and only because I had a thriving real estate business and income to fall back on if needed, I finally gained the courage to file a formal grievance against a supervisor. I was fed up and tired of how I had been treated for years.

I had kept documentation for years that included text messages, personal notes, photos, recordings, but especially emails. And I presented all of this information to my HR department. Though I cannot go into specific detail regarding the final outcome, I can say that I feel I had not received any recourse. This was expected based on experiences that other professors had endured and shared with me.

But a supervisor "retired" shortly after my grievance, so perhaps that was some sort of recourse or relief. I did not find the retirement to be a mere coincidence either, as many of us knew that supervisor had not planned on retiring for several more years. I still thought it was BS! Bad supervisors had mistreated others as well with no recourse which forced some employees to simply quit or retire. Sad.

Others quit and sued the college claiming civil rights violations that pertained to age and gender discrimination, violation of the Family Medical Leave Act (FMLA), disability discrimination, retaliation for requesting reasonable accommodations in violation of Section 504 of the Rehabilitation Act, the Oklahoma Discrimination in Employment Act, as reported by the Pioneer Newspaper which is the college newspaper at OCCC. I put my failed grievance attempt behind me and moved on.

Despite the COVID-19 pandemic that plagued the world, 2020 was my best year yet in terms of real estate, and it would also place me in a position as a whistle-blower, so to speak, to affect significant change at Oklahoma City Community College by highlighting the history of a perceived punitive and retaliatory culture and those responsible for perpetuating it. But let's start with real estate.

CHAPTER SIX

2020

I was blessed and fortunate to close on seventy-one homes. It was a great year! The pandemic sent the real estate industry into a frenzy which turned the real estate market into a year-long seller's market, as the historically-low interest rates created this huge influx of buyers. And buyers were buying at a rate faster than sellers were or could list their homes for sale. This created extremely low inventory.

Sellers were winning, so to speak, because low inventory means that there are fewer available homes on the market for sale which means there is less competition for sellers that translates into sellers receiving multiple offers over the asking price, not having to pay any of the buyer's closing costs, all within 24 to 48 hours. Absolutely crazy market!

Buyers were winning with the low-interest rates and sellers were winning by selling their homes over market value and maximizing their net/profit. But while this COVID-19 market was booming, as the months passed, buyers were beginning to feel the adverse effects of the market.

For example, the day that I listed a home for sale, I would have on average about 20 to 25 showings and receive about 15 to 20 offers. The multiple-offer situation turned into a bidding war. And the seller can only accept one of the offers. That means the other 19 buyers who submitted an offer lost out and had to start the home search and viewing process all over again. This process could take days, weeks, or even months as homes were selling faster than buyers could schedule to view them.

I do not know how many times I had my buyers contact me to schedule a showing for a home that just hit the market and before I could get my showing/viewing request confirmed by the seller's agent, I would be notified that the sellers had already accepted an offer. Crazy!

This became very common throughout the entire U.S. market, at least based on my experiences with my clients and several other agents who had shared similar experiences. And I was also seeing this across the nation as well on the nightly news. So I had to be strategic with my buyers. There were some tips and strategies that I used that helped several of my buyers finally go under contract with a home. I will share them in my upcoming real estate book.

Nevertheless, my tips and strategies were working for several of my buyers but unfortunately not all of them. And many of them began to get frustrated, exhausted and stressed out over the process which is something that I was not used to, as all of my 5-star reviews and testimonials commonly state how much fun I made the process for them. But those reviews were pre-COVID-19.

Some of my buyers ended up taking a break for a few weeks or months and some of them decided to go and build a custom home. At least if they went that route, they did not have to worry about competing against 20 other buyers trying to buy the same home. And builders were winning as well, as they were seeing this influx of buyers shifting to building because they simply could not secure an existing home based on the current market.

Despite the pandemic, my business was still growing, so much so, that I hired a full-time assistant to join my team. It was me, my Transaction Coordinator, and an assistant. And this team of three was blessed and humbled to serve and assist these 71 families. And I truly mean blessed, as there were hundreds, if not thousands of real estate agents, who left the industry because they were not able to produce. The pandemic was extremely good for many, but very bad for others as well. I was blessed.

And my extended "team members" had closed on about fifteen additional homes. They were growing as well and I could not wait for what the following year had in store for them.

Though 2020 was an amazing year for me in regards to real estate, it was also a fulfilling year for me as well, as I would be the catalyst that would affect significant change at OCCC. Had the next set of events not taken place, I truly believed that I would have either been terminated or quit as a full-time professor of sixteen years.

As I previously mentioned, OCCC had a history of a very punitive and retaliatory culture. Just over my tenure of sixteen years, I witnessed dozens of faculty, staff, and employees experience what I perceived as being targeted, harassed, and discriminated against by supervisors and administrators without any relief or recourse being provided by our HR department.

Our HR department was not an HR department, as the final decisions, especially in regards to formal grievances filed against supervisors, were decided by administrators. The very administrators who were the boss of those supervisors. Biased?? Uh, yea! And the college policies that were in place put faculty, staff, and employees at a very significant disadvantage – all of which would be acknowledged and validated by a new executive team of administrators during several listening sessions that were held on campus for faculty, staff, and employees to attend and ask questions and voice our concerns. These sessions were released to the public on YouTube in an effort by the new Executive Team to be transparent.

For years, as I watched so many of my OCCC family members be clinically diagnosed with stress, anxiety, depression, PTSD, etc., at the hands of bad supervisors and administrators, I decided to make a move and come forward to do something about this punitive and retaliatory culture. The last straw came when I believed I had become yet another victim and was retaliated against by a supervisor for having something to do with a previous supervisor's "retirement."

And when I thought I had gotten rid of a previous bad supervisor just a few months prior, I felt I was now being targeted and retaliated against by a new supervisor, who just so happened to be the supervisor, colleague, and friend of the previous supervisor who had "retired." See the connection?

For sixteen years, I had stellar performance evaluation reviews that determined whether I would receive a salary increase based on fulfilling my duties and responsibilities to the college. I was now, for the first time *ever*, being marked as partially fulfilling my duties and responsibilities. Not a coincidence. Not a surprise either.

On September 17, 2020, I was fed up and posted an emotional 5-minute video on my Facebook page, as well as other social media outlets, that explained some of my previous subliminal posts regarding OCCC. You see, over the past year or so, I began posting references to bad supervisors, punitive and retaliatory cultures, etc. but never naming the college directly. I also posted the video to let everyone know about my experiences and true struggles at the college. The video went viral with thousands of views and hundreds of comments from current and former faculty, staff, and employees just within a few hours of posting.

I posted this video fully knowing the consequences that I may face which was possible termination by the college. But, I. DID. NOT. CARE. I was traumatized. I was mentally, physically, and spiritually broken and exhausted due to the years of what I perceived as harassment, targeting, retaliation, and discrimination. I was also being the voice for so many other faculty, staff, and employees, who had reached out to me over the previous months to share their horrible experiences that were very similar to mine. I received a TON of support.

The stories that were shared brought me to tears. And these victims did not have a voice as they were ALL afraid to come forward. They saw what happened to those who came forward to file complaints or grievances against a supervisor or administrator. They were either terminated or were harassed and targeted even more according to them.

Many of these victims did not have the luxury of a second career that provided financial stability like I had. These victims were older, some were near retirement, some did not have any other job experience, making it difficult to find another job in higher education. Jobs in higher education are already difficult to obtain, so many of these victims simply kept quiet and endured. Some of them were in pretty bad shape sharing how they were in therapy, taking anti-depressants, clinically diagnosed with PTSD, becoming physically nauseous when driving up to campus for work, and more. I posted their comments on my social media with their permission, of course, and kept them confidential by redacting names, per their request, as some of them were afraid of continued or additional retaliation by supervisors, administrators, and the college[21]. I had to be a voice for them as well. They were my friends. They were my *family*.

I was not afraid anymore and I had my successful real estate business to thank for that as it provided me a platform to affect change. My business provided me financial stability and the courage needed to speak out against the college. I was now on a mission to affect change. I afforded administration and supervisors plenty of opportunities to do the right thing just in my grievances and complaints alone over the years and they ignored me. They had messed with the wrong person. *For a full summary and update of the entire process, simply watch my YouTube video titled: "Recap and Update Regarding the Chaos and*

---

[21] See photos #18 and 19

Culture at Oklahoma City Community College." It's quite good, I believe, with graphics, and photos.

For the sake of brevity, I have provided a summary of what transpired and the significant changes the college implemented just a few weeks after my initial social media post on September 17th, 2020 through March of 2021[22].

I set the wheels in motion on September 17, 2020, and trusted the new Chief of Staff (now Executive Vice President) would fulfill her promise in making significant change. And though I was hesitant, she acted swiftly and made a lot of significant changes by January of 2021. And she is still making changes as I am writing this now.

I was extremely proud of the change I helped to bring to the college and my OCCC family, but there's no way that I could have done this without the support from everyone. Professor Markus Zindelo, the very brave adviser for the Pioneer Newspaper and its published stories played a significant role as well, as they were relentless in printing stories and updates each week highlighting the movement for change. The countless others who came forward to share their similar stories were significant as well, as they corroborated and validated my reasons and actions for this movement for change. And I call it a movement because it was.

It reminds me of Dr. Martin Luther King's words: "Nonviolent direct action seeks to create such a crisis and foster such a tension that a community which has constantly refused to negotiate is forced to confront the issue." And we, myself, faculty, staff, and employees, fostered such a tension to finally compel the college to confront the issue.

Real estate was my superhero cape, so to speak, because with it, I was no longer scared or concerned about the likelihood that I would be terminated by the college for speaking out against them. Real estate

---

[22] See Appendix #4

afforded me the courage and voice to affect change to help rescue others.

CHAPTER SEVEN

LESSONS LEARNED

Overall, my real estate journey has been a wonderful experience. I love that I get to make dreams a reality for so many families. The looks on my buyers' faces when they are officially handed the keys to their new home is PRICELESS! And the looks on my sellers' faces when they receive their check for thousands of dollars over what they were expecting is also PRICELESS!

What I have learned over the years, and I truly believe that it has led to my success, is that I never got into real estate for the money. You know the main reason why I got into real estate, but beyond that, I got into real estate because I wanted to change and impact lives. In a way similar to how I have impacted thousands of students that I have been fortunate enough to teach in the college classroom.

Even after nineteen years of teaching as a professor of political science, I still receive text messages, emails, phone calls, social media comments, and messages from students thanking me for sharing a little bit of my story, my journey with them. I heard from a former student just the other day. They were in one of my courses ten years ago, and let me know that they had recently graduated from law school. They said they owed it all to me as I planted the seed some years ago when they were a student sitting in my classroom.

Each time I receive news like this from a former student, I always feel like a very proud father, as I transform the classroom into a community and the students become family. And consistently receiving news like this over the years confirms for me that I am continuing to do the right things in the classroom with my students, who become like *family*. And this family aspect relationship that I have with my students flows directly into my real estate, as I have been blessed to be able to assist many of my former students in buying their first home. PRICELESS!

This was the impact that I wanted to have with my real estate clients; changing lives. And I believe I have done that by never focusing on the money, but solely on the relationships. As my motto with my team goes: "Never chase the money! Chase the relationships!" If you chase the relationships the money will come. And I mean that sincerely. But don't get me wrong, the money is great!

Here are some words of wisdom to some of the new real estate agents and even experienced real estate agents. If you focus on the relationships first and take great care of your clients, guess what they will do? They will continue to use you as their real estate agent and tell all of their family and friends about you who will also utilize your services. My business is 95% referral-based. I cannot tell you how many families and friends I have assisted with my initial relationship with a client.

For example, I had one family where I assisted Mom and Dad to sell their current home and then helped them buy a new home. Then, their daughter and son-in-law used me to sell their current home and help them buy a new home. Then, their son and daughter-in-law used me to help them purchase a home. For this one family, I was able to assist in the buying and selling of a total of five homes just based on my initial relationship with Mom and Dad. And all of them continue to refer me to their friends.

The problem I have seen over the years are agents who live by a different creed. They focus on the money first and never on the relationship. The stories I have heard from other agents and clients who had been duped or forced to purchase a home that they really could not afford or purchase a home that required a lot of major repairs but were convinced to purchase and close on the home anyways. That's putting money first and it's wrong on so many levels.

But what those agents did in putting money first was to completely ruin and sever the relationship and potential for growing their business because they put their clients in a horrible position, and I can guarantee you that they will never use that agent again. And their loss has been my gain, as those clients come to me and other real estate agents wanting to utilize our services.

But at the end of the day, I will not judge those agents. I do not know what is going on in their lives that may be influencing their decisions to not focus on the relationship and the best interest of their clients. I just know that money has never been a driving factor for me. Never will be. This could also be due to my upbringing, as I was just happy to have the bare necessities in life.

Growing up in poverty and in the 'hoods I grew up in, I believe humbles you. Humbles you to appreciate the small things in life. Don't get me wrong, I do tend to splurge from time to time on an occasional pair of Vans. I mean, come on! I am known as the Suits and Vans Realtor Man on Instagram, YouTube, Facebook, and even TikTok. I do drive a Mercedes SUV, but I have been driving those even before I got into real estate. I purchased my first Mercedes C300 sedan back in 2006 when I landed my first "adult" job as a tenured professor. Oh, best believe it was the cheapest base model at $30,000, but it was brand new and I was proud.

That purchase meant a lot to me because as a kid, we always had gang members and drug dealers driving through our 'hoods in a

Mercedes or BMW, and I told myself that one day, I didn't know when, and I didn't know how, but I was going to buy me a Mercedes the legal way. With career money and not drug or gang money.

Other than my suits, Vans, watches, and my SUV, I live a pretty modest life. I could easily afford to buy a million-dollar home if I wanted, but instead, I choose to live in a 2000 square foot home that I had built back in 2014.

Though I could splurge and indulge more with the wealth that I have been so blessed to have acquired solely from real estate, I prefer to spend the bulk of my earnings giving back to the community. The proceeds from this book are going to local charities and scholarships, so know that your purchase will help others and communities in need as discussed in a previous chapter.

I truly enjoy giving back to my community. I tell people all the time that I was placed here on this earth for a reason and purpose. And I believe that was to be a giver and provider for those who were struggling in their lives and just needed that extra little bit of help.

This so resonates with me as I recall the reaction from the carhop at the Sonic Drive-in when I tipped her $100 for a $2.19 drink order. She broke down in tears. She was an older lady and I had been going to this place for years. She was always there and was always so kind; just a very sweet person. When she told me that her apartment had just burned down and she had been sleeping in her car for the past couple of days and that $100 tip arrived at the best time, I knew what was taking place was much bigger than the two of us at that moment. She was extremely grateful and it had this extremely profound effect on me. Real estate allowed me to do this.

Another example that brings tears to my eyes every time I think about it or share the story is when I was having this really bad day dealing with lenders, title companies, etc. I was headed out to do a final walkthrough of a home and was about an hour or so ahead of schedule, so I stopped at a local restaurant on my way for a quick bite to kill a little bit of time. I was so stressed out by the day and putting out fires that I had a massive headache. I walked into the restaurant and was greeted by the sweet hostess. Despite this throbbing headache, I still managed to be nice and polite to the hostess as she was walking me to my booth. I took my seat. The server quickly came to my table to take my drink order. She was just the sweetest person with this great upbeat attitude and just smiling the entire time.

I informed her that I was a little bit in a hurry, so if we could get my order in as soon as possible that would be great. Her attitude and behavior brought about this sense of calm that resonated throughout my entire body. And by the time she had taken my order, my headache was going away. A few minutes passed and I was already receiving my food. She went out of her way to accommodate my short window of time and even left my check with me as soon as she placed my food in front of me saying, "I know you are in a hurry, so I am going to leave this check with you now so you do not have to wait on me. Also, as I see you finishing up your meal, I will bring you a to-go drink as you head out."

I was blown away by her and the service. And trust me, I know great service when I see it. But I was more blown away just by her kind nature. Just before I had finished off my grilled chicken, I had placed my credit card on the table on top of the check and within a minute, she was swooping by to collect the card and check. She quickly came back and by this point, my headache was completely gone. She handed me my check and card and thanked me for coming in today and walked away. Once again, she was as pleasant as could be.

I flagged down one of the other servers and asked to speak to her manager. The manager approached my booth and I could already see the paranoid look on her face, as they believed they were most likely going to get a tongue-lashing and complaint. But I immediately told the manager how very pleased I was with my server and told her that she should know that. I then asked the manager to have the server come back by as I had something to give her. When my server arrived, I thanked her again for the awesome service but more importantly, I told her that she turned my bad day into a great day and that she made me feel so much better. I then handed her the check.

She picked it up and saw the $100 tip and said, "You aren't serious, are you?" I told her, "Yes, I am." "Oh, my goodness!" she squealed. And it was at that moment that I think it *really* hit her and she began to cry. I stood up and gave her a great big hug and thanked her once again. She explained to me how she so desperately needed this tip today. I told her that it was my pleasure and that what she did for me in that 30 minutes was priceless. Real estate allowed me to do this.

Three years later, guess what? The server contacted me to let me know that she and her husband were finally in a financial position to buy their first home and there was no one else they would ever consider working with but me. Remember my previous discussion on building relationships and not chasing the money? Well, there ya go.

I was so grateful to assist them in purchasing their first home and it was a gorgeous updated home. I was so very proud of them. Just three years prior, they were having financial difficulties and not so great credit and now here they were buying their dream home. There were some tears shed at closing.

It's events like this that serve as a constant reminder that I believe I was placed here for a purpose. I mean, statistics say that I should have been either incarcerated or dead as a black male growing up, especially in the 'hood back in the 70s, 80s, and 90s. And when I think about all of the bad things that I had done during those times, and all of the bad things that I had avoided, especially during my 20s, I believe there was a higher power or force truly watching over me. I truly believe this.

Real estate has been extremely good to me and I have never taken it for granted. Just to be doing real estate going on 6 years now is truly a testament, as research data has indicated that roughly 85% of all real estate agents fail in the first 5 years and end up leaving the industry. But I have been one of the lucky ones and this is attributed to hundreds of families that I have been able to assist over the years, the thousands of social media friends, and close friends, and family's support.

I would not be in the position I am in right now had it not been for their support and especially referrals. The best advice I can give any new agent or someone thinking about getting into real estate is to establish a strong foundation for referrals. Let me explain.

I am especially known in the real estate industry due to my honesty, integrity, and excellent customer service. But more importantly, all of my clients are made to feel like *family* throughout the entire process. I do not know how many times I have seen "family" mentioned in feedback, reviews, text messages that I have received from my clients, who truly become friends and family for life.

This sense of family is a powerful tool, and I mean "tool" most sincerely and organically. When you treat your clients like family means you are putting their best interest above anything else, especially your commission check. For example, I have talked several of my buyers over the years out of buying a home that I would not let my parents, daughter, son, or anyone else close to me purchase. Of course, I can only provide my recommendations when requested, as, at the end of the day, it is the client's final decision.

At times, I have explained to my clients in the initial process that I will be that objective voice of reason and will be open and honest with them. And they appreciate that. They often tell me that is one of the main reasons they specifically reached out to me, as they heard about my honesty and integrity from a friend or family member or viewed one of my Smith Talk Tuesday episodes on my YouTube channel: Suits and Vans Realtor Man.

Many clients, whether buyers or sellers, go into the real estate process with emotions and it's my job to be that objective voice of reason and at times protecting my clients from themselves. But that veil of protection that I provide strikes at the heart of that sense of *family* that I also provide to all of my clients.

At the end of every closing, I always tell my clients, "Welcome to the Markus Smith Real Estate Team family!" And that resonates with them. And I mean what I say, because I will always be in touch with them, reaching out every couple of months via text, email, phone calls, or especially through social media to wish them Happy Birthday, Happy Anniversary, It's Daylight Savings Day, Wishing You a Speedy Recovery, Happy Easter, Happy Thanksgiving, Merry Christmas, or any other reason I can have to just stay in contact with them.

As I mentioned before, real estate has been very good to me, and I do not take it for granted. But, for the record, I have worked my ass off, too. I knew that I was going to do great in real estate. I did! How do I know that? Because I just had to be great. In other words, I have always attacked every endeavor with the mindset of being the absolute best, whether that was my journey on bettering my life and escaping from the 'hood and its activities, or whether that was achieving the highest academic degree possible in a Ph.D., or whether it was achieving success in real estate. I attacked it!

Failure has never been an option for me. The hustling and grinding mentality that I have always had I attribute to my mother as her hard work has always served as inspiration and motivation. Nevertheless, I firmly believe that to be successful in life, you have to have that mentality – that is, you will do whatever it takes to be the very best and accomplish all of your goals.

It's Sunday, May 2, 2021, and as I sit here and wrap up part 3 of my memoir, I do not know what the future holds for me in my real estate endeavors. Will I continue the hustle and grind and constant chaos that comes along with being a top-producing real estate agent? I am not sure. Staying as busy as I have been is a blessing, but it's also a curse.

CHAPTER EIGHT

LISTEN UP

Listen up new real estate agents, or those thinking about getting into real estate. Real estate can take a toll on you, your family, and your friends, as you are constantly on the go or on the phone talking, texting, social media posting, and emailing.

Also, get used to getting up at 6 am, leaving the house by 8 am, and not getting back home until 10 pm. And even after you get home, you will find yourselves working until midnight or later, as real estate DOES NOT STOP! That is the life of a top-producer. But I have always said that you get as much out of real estate as you put into it.

I will turn the "big 50" in about two months and I am starting to look at life a little differently now. This may also be due to the COVID-19 pandemic that has plagued all of us for over a year now. It has put things in a different perspective for me.

I finally saw my parents and nephew, Anthony, for dinner the other evening. This was the first time in well over a year that I had seen the three of them due to COVID-19. My parents are now in their 70s, so I had been extremely careful not to visit them due to my COVID-19 fears. It was great to finally see them for dinner. I missed them.

I have seen so many people affected by this pandemic. I have had close friends die due to the coronavirus. I have seen my friends' family members die due to coronavirus. Coronavirus has torn families apart in the past year, and it has me thinking about the more important things in life: family.

I miss Nikki as well, as I have not seen her in more than a year. She is doing extremely well navigating through life and taking great care of my grandson. I definitely miss her face and see she is looking more and more like my mom – or her "nana" as Nikki has always called her. As Nikki gets older, I believe the Asian gene is coming through more and more like it did with me, but Nikki does not see it. Typical 29-year-old. But you be the judge[23].

I also have my four-year-old grandson, Greyson-Markus[24], who lives in Colorado that I would love to be able to spend more time with. He calls me "Doc" by the way, as I am by no means a "papa" or "grandpa" in any sense of the word or the perception that goes along with it. Plus, he already has his "papa" or "grandpa" because my father, who is Greyson's great-grandfather, is still alive and doing well.

So to minimize any confusion with Greyson and to differentiate between me and my father and his other grandfather in Colorado (Nikki's stepdad), he learned at an early age to call me "Doc" as it's fitting because a lot of people call me "Dr. Smith", and it's cute because it makes people around us giggle when they hear him call me "Doc." But I haven't seen him or my daughter in over a year due to COVID-19.

Between my real estate business and other commitments, and especially due to the COVID-19 pandemic, it's been extremely challenging to spend time with him and with my family in general. But I know some of that is my fault because I have chosen work over family

---

[23] See photo #20
[24] See photos #21 and 22

for the past few years as I was growing my real estate business, and it took a toll on my marriage as well.

For years I have tried to listen to my work wife, Kaitlin, who is a good friend and Escrow Closer/Manager at Chicago Title Oklahoma Nichols Hills. She has been telling me for years that I need to find a way to take a break from real estate, even if it's just for a weekend. Being a top-producer herself in her own field, I see all of the time how she takes trips with friends and family and just enjoying some down time. I asked her despite having the same chaotic work schedule as me, how she is able to find that balance in taking breaks, vacations, etc. Her response is always: "you just have to make time. You have to do it for your well-being and your family." But despite these friendly conversations with Kaitlin over the years, I have yet been able to take her advice.

But with more and more people getting vaccinated, the rates of COVID-19 declining, my real estate business running like a well-oiled machine, my health is great, my finances are in order, and turning the big 50 in a couple of months, it appears that my priorities are shifting. It's time to enjoy life and family more, especially with my 4-legged babies: Pedro and McGee, who are always so excited and happy to see me which instantly turns a bad day into a good one[25]. I mean, all have been neglected as they have taken a backseat to real estate.

Though family is extremely important, unfortunately, I had to make some sacrifices for me and my family. And that sacrifice was due to real estate. For the first couple of years into my real estate career, my family had taken a backseat because I wanted to work my ass off, hustling and grinding and building my real estate business so that my family and I would be in a better place in our lives. I often say, "I work hard now so I do not have to later." Please do not get me wrong, real estate has done so much for me as you already know. I am not here to bash or criticize real estate or anything because it was my decisions that put real estate first for years. But I have always told others, what is the

---

[25] See photo #23

point of making and having all of this money if you do not have the time to share it with the ones you love. It's time I start taking my own advice.

I definitely enjoyed writing this memoir, so who knows, perhaps I will publish more books in the future. I know that I will begin writing another book soon solely based on real estate. I want to share tips and strategies that have been extremely successful for me, my other "team members", and other real estate agents and brokers I have provided information to over the years.

Over these past 6 years of doing real estate, there have been hundreds of real estate agents and brokers (new and experienced), as well as those who are thinking about getting into real estate, who have reached out to me to share my tips and strategies that have led to my successes.

And I do not mind sharing that information at all, despite real estate being a very cutthroat industry, unfortunately. (And to the "Karen" real estate agents out there, there is entirely too much real estate out there for you to act petty! Be better. Do better. Real estate does not have to be cutthroat).

Stay tuned my fellow real estate agents, brokers, and those interested in getting into real estate, as another book is in the works.

I hope my journey in real estate that I have shared with you helps to put some things in perspective. For those who are interested in getting into real estate, I have provided some of my experiences and the expectations regarding real estate as raw and honest as possible, because I want you to know exactly what you are getting yourselves into.

And to the new and experienced real estate agents and brokers, I am hopeful that what little information I have shared has made you take a step back and re-evaluate and put things in perspective as well.

What I have learned, however, is even though I have only been doing real estate for 6 years, I have been blessed enough to have done more business transactions than a great deal of other real estate agents who have been in the business for more than 20 years. I believe that my tips and strategies do have some value for others to benefit from despite my short time in real estate.

And to those that question me and have the mindset of "who the hell does this guy think he is?" – I am clearly not talking to you, as you have obviously missed the message I have tried to convey. I am talking to those who have read my memoir and know that the information I am providing is sincere and is coming from a good place.

I am sharing my real estate wisdom in hopes that it will help you grow your business, find yourselves, but more importantly, finding that happy medium in balancing work and family. I have yet to see a chapter in a real estate book/manual that discusses the importance of balancing real estate and family, so hopefully, this memoir will be a great start for you, as well as future books that may be in the works.

With that being said, who knows what my future has in store for me? I know that I will be taking a step back from real estate. How far back, I simply do not know. You already know how I am wired, though.

A FINAL WORD...

I am often asked how I managed to get 'out'. What was it that helped me decide to do more with my life? This isn't a question that's easily answered, and the answer is multifaceted.

Seeing so many people I knew and cared about gunned down in the streets through gang activity throughout my childhood and teen years certainly affected me. Seeing my friends in and out of jail was also a great deterrent to that lifestyle. But still, for many people who grew up just like me, these events only lent themselves to more anger and a tendency to stay in the 'hood out of a feeling of obligation and loyalty.

My mom certainly wanted more for me. She invested so much of her own time into building that work ethic in me. Mom was always telling me how far I could go if I would just get a good education. She was aware of my activities, but she never really busted me for them. I think she knew that in some aspect, I was still a product of my environment and all she could do was love me fiercely and guide me the best she could. I distinctly remember a time mom came out to my car and saw my gun sitting on my passenger seat. For most parents, this would have been a moment to freak out, start a long line of questioning. Mom didn't say a word.

So, what was it that set me on a different path? How was it that I ended up with custody of my daughter, with a Ph.D., and a successful career path while a lot of my homeboys ended up remaining in the 'hood, in and out of jail, and sticking with that lifestyle? The answer is twofold.

First, the most important reason I can come up with when asked this question is familial culture. Often in black families, at age 18, you're an adult and it's time to get out on your own. I believe this was definitely my dad's mentality and the reason why he had grown so angry with me over the years that led up to our last physical altercation which resulted in me finally moving out at the age of 26 or 27. In fairness, it probably didn't help that I had often been coming home drunk with girls, juggling jobs, no college degree, getting in trouble, and so much more.

However, in Asian families, generational living is considered normal. There are often 3 or more generations living together. My mom was in no hurry to get me out of the house. It was her love and guidance that allowed me to appreciate what I had with the Poos family when I finally moved out.

While I didn't spend a ton of time at home as a teen, I always knew I had my parents at home for me. Not everyone had such a support system due to single-parent homes. Single moms had to work two, sometimes three jobs. This didn't allow for them to be present when kids needed them most. They were busy making sure rent was paid, electricity was on, food was on the table and everyone had what they needed. This isn't to say they weren't doing a good job – they were! They were doing what had to be done. It also meant kids were raising themselves or relying on others such as gang members, family, or neighborhood moms to raise them.

In that way, I was privileged. I didn't know it at the time but even growing up in the same neighborhood, I was granted a different cultural experience than even my closest of friends. In some cases, even my same family members.

Second, I was extremely blessed and fortunate to be surrounded by so many people beyond my parents – an extended family, if you will –

who loved and cared for my well-being and future. Whether it was my 'hood moms during my early years, "moms" and "pops" during my 20s, the Poos family, extended Poos families, and all of my mentors during my 30s, I had these people in my life who kept me grounded and on a path to success. I will forever be grateful to each and every one of them.

I never in a million years thought I would be comfortable enough to share my journeys with you. For the past 20 years or so when I first began sharing my story to my mentors and then later with my students and at-risk adults and children, I was always told, "you should write a book." I would always kindly laugh it off and change the subject.

But as the years passed, and I was sharing a little bit of my story with more and more people, I would often have these same people contacting me years later telling me how my story inspired and motivated them. And saved them in some instances.

I continued to fight with my own emotions in being comfortable to share my story, even though I had all of these people whose lives I had been impacting with my story, but I had this perceived low value of my self-worth and importance. They call it being humble, which I feel I have always been.

But I had always believed that writing a book and sharing my story was something only arrogant people did. "Hey, look at me and how successful I am!" But of course, I let my ignorance blind me, as I discovered that when someone writes an autobiography or memoir, it's all about the intent.

Yes, thousands of authors write "Look at me and all of my accomplishments!" types of books, but there are also other authors who write from the heart. That is what I have attempted to do as well.

Nevertheless, I fought the push from my students, mentors, and others to write and publish my story. I just could not get past feeling like a very arrogant person. I just could not do it. But as more years passed and I received more and more testimonials from people with who I had shared my story, I was finally feeling more comfortable in entertaining the idea. I mentioned to many of my family and close friends my thoughts on writing a memoir. And something that resonated with all of them was that if my story had impacted hundreds of former and current students over the years, just imagine how many others outside of my inner circle in Oklahoma could be impacted as well.

I vividly remember being told, "You owe it to yourself and others to share your story. Think about how many thousands and perhaps millions of people are out there right now who need to hear your story. Your story will save lives, Markus."

This compelled me. Despite my reservations, my story needed to be told. I was still afraid, though, as I knew that sharing my journey meant sharing the good and the bad. And there was a lot of bad.

I was afraid, especially for my successful real estate business that I spent years working tirelessly to build. Would some of my clients be upset about my past? Would some judge me? Would I lose some of those relationships? I believed the answer was: yes. However, my thoughts were that if I lost any clients, or friends for that matter, then they were probably people I did not want to have a relationship with anyways. Those who truly knew and understood me would still support me.

Sharing my story was much bigger than me worrying about losing clients or friends. And though my status in life may have significantly changed, my heart and love for people have always remained the same. This is what finally compelled me to move forward in writing and sharing my journey with you. So, last year, I decided to finally put pen to paper, or should I say fingers to keyboard, and began the process.

First and foremost, know what you want for yourself. Find a way to immerse yourself in something positive. For me, that was taekwondo. Realize that if you are coming from a place of poverty and violence, that education is going to be your ticket out. Do you need to pursue a PhD? Of course not. But take your education seriously. Present yourself as an educated human. It will truly open doors for you.

If I can get myself out of the gangster 'hood and into the Ph.D. hood, so can you! Don't let anyone convince you that you *must* become a product of your environment. Don't allow yourself to become convinced that you're somehow stuck. Don't believe you are being disloyal by getting out and taking care of yourself. Quite the contrary! By being and becoming the best version of you, it will allow you to remain loyal and to give back to those who have always been there for you.

I hope that my journey serves to inspire and motivate you regardless of what adversity or hardships you may be facing. Regardless of what demons you may be battling. Regardless of what life may have thrown at you. You will persevere. You have to! And I believe in you! Life is a journey and though many of you may have had the odds stacked against you, you have to rise above it all and pave the way for others who need to hear your story as well.

So please accept my story as a gift in hopes that it will change your life and the lives of those you will impact, for the better.

APPENDIX

Item #1: Email to the Secretary, Ph.D. and Graduate Students
Tracy,

After careful consideration, I have decided to pursue a different path with my studies, despite the fact that I was only one course (POL 5950) away from taking general exams this semester. I have been accepted into another Ph.D. program that not only supports my teaching career, but has done more mentoring with me in a few weeks than the four years that I have spent in the Political Science program. This new program also lacks the egocentric nature that is prevalent among many of the professors that I have encountered in your department.

I will say, however, that I truly appreciated how Drs. Franklin, Raadschelders, and Givel were always there for me and served in a capacity that many of the other faculty members will never be able to grasp or comprehend. A great deal can be learned from these three professors.

I also want you to know that I appreciate everything that you have done for me during the past couple of years, but the politics and jumping through hoops, so to speak, is just not what I signed up for. In other words, I am not a "traditional" Ph.D. student who can dedicate their entire life to the department. For one, I am not a kid; I am 37 years old with many responsibilities (i.e., a family, children, and a full-time teaching career which many of the students within the program are striving for). And because I am not a "traditional" Ph.D. student, I continue to be penalized. In other words, there is a double-standard for "traditional" versus non-"traditional" students. I had been forewarned about the political science department from many colleagues, mentors, students, and friends from various institutions, but decided to pursue the program nonetheless.

I truly understand that a Ph.D. is something that takes a lot of discipline, dedication, and hard work. I also understand that going through the process of obtaining a Ph.D. is a "rite of passage," so to speak. But I have persevered through more adversity from this program than any disciplined, dedicated, and hard-working student should have to endure. You would think that the department would realize that as a non-"traditional" student, I have had to work twice as hard. You would also think that the department would have embraced and supported the fact that I am teaching full-time, but that has never been the case. It was even suggested early on that I quit my full-time teaching job to work in the department. To this day I still do not comprehend that.

I know that this correspondence may fall on deaf ears and some will say that had I just been able to spend more time on campus and within the department, I would not feel the way that I do. I know that others will also feel that I have this all wrong and that I am the one misperceiving everything about the department. These reactions will not be too unexpected due to the egocentric nature that I alluded to earlier. There are other various Ph.D. programs on campus that are just as competitive, rigorous, and scholarly as political science, but they actually mentor and support all of their students, regardless if they are "traditional" or non-"traditional."

Your department has a reputation that is not to be proud of and I am hoping that this may change soon so that I will be able to speak highly of it to my students who may be interested in pursuing a political science degree.

Well, Tracy, I believe that I have pontificated quite long enough. I want to thank you, once again, especially for trying to convince me over the break to stay with the program. Though this new program will set me back about a year and a half, I know I will be happier. Lastly, know that I am not the only student in your program who feels this way. There are several others, but they choose to abstain in fear of retaliation, so I have spoken for them as well.

Item #2: Dissertation Abstract

There exists a culture of surviving victims who possess a body of knowledge stemming from their experiences of dealing with homicide. In reviewing the literature on surviving victims, whether they are survivors of the victim (Master et al. 1987) or the accused (Sharp 2005), it is evident that their diverse views are often unrealized or ignored by the very citizens and policymakers responsible for initiating and evaluating criminal justice policies (King 2003; Armour 2002; Thompson et al. 1998; Kilpatrick et al. 1990). Ignoring this group, perhaps those who could contribute most to the dialogue surrounding criminal justice policy, limits the body of cultural knowledge which can be transmitted and used to educate the citizenry, thereby resulting in producing a flawed public policy that, ultimately, negatively impacts citizens and the entire nation (Constantine 2000). The "transmission" of informed knowledge and "cultural wealth," as posited in John Dewey's *Democracy and Education* (1916) and Jane Roland Martin's *Cultural Miseducation* (2002), is crucial because an informed citizenry is essential for any democracy to thrive.

Though the transmission of knowledge is important, this study primarily serves as an educative instrument by producing a body of cultural knowledge to enrich the lived experiences of six surviving victims and to convey their growth from the tragic event. The collective growth from tragedy serves an educative and democratic purpose, because it mends the knowledge gap by informing and increasing public awareness which, in turn, dissolves public ignorance and ensures equity in the creation of effective and successful policy. The researcher believes that his position as a professor at a community college affords him the opportunity to go beyond an academic community and to reach and carry out this educative process (in the spirit of Dewey and Martin) to average citizens as well – or, non-traditional students who are working-class adults who oftentimes occupy an unentitled status.

A series of interviews, journal notes, audio recordings, and transcriptions were used to collect the data for this interpretive phenomenological study. van Manen's (1990) phenomenological methodology provides an etic overlay with which to understand the participants' existential lifeworlds: temporality (lived time), spatiality (lived space), relationality (lived relation), and corporeality (lived body). This process initiates the peeling back of the layers of reflection to expose the participants' growth from tragedy. Based on the findings, three thematic categories emerged from the lived experiences: validity of the criminal justice system and the death penalty, finding peace or closure, and the impact of the southern region and Oklahoma. The thematic categories ultimately reveal how each participant has grown from a tragedy which, more importantly, informs citizens about a need for changes in how public opinion polls are used to evaluate the validity of criminal justice policies, especially death penalty policy.

The significance of the study calls for future research to enrich the understanding of how surviving victims have been affected by tragedy and then to use that cultural knowledge to educate others, whether it be other surviving victims, research scholars, policymakers, media, uninformed citizens, etc. To be informed is essential for the success of a democratic state (Mill 1859; Barber 1995; Lau & Redlawsk 1997), being that the majority's views prevail, which influences the direction of government and public policy.

Item #3: Awards and Accolades

Some prestigious academic and teaching awards I have received throughout my journey include:

Phi Theta Kappa International Honor Society;
Certificate of Achievement Presented by Oklahoma City Community College.
Oklahoma City Community College Alumni Hall of Fame;
"Award for Teaching" by the American Association of University Professors;
"Great Ideas for Teaching Award" by the Oklahoma Association of Community Colleges;
"Celebration of Education 'Outstanding Educator' Award" – one of the highest honors that the Jeannine Rainbolt College of Education awards for educators by the University of Oklahoma;
National Dean's List; Pi Sigma Alpha (Political Science Honor Society);
Golden Key International Honour Society;
President's and Dean's Honor Roll;
American Political Science Association Award;
Political Science Student Leadership Award;
Multicultural Student Services Academic Achievement Award;
Pi Sigma Alpha "National Best Chapter Award" as President;
College of Liberal Arts Outstanding Graduate Student;
John & Eleanor Kirkpatrick Student Leadership & Public Service Award;
Political Science Department's Outstanding Graduate Student Award;
Who's Who Among Students in American Universities and Colleges

Item #4: OCCC Timeline of Change

1). With the help of the Pioneer Newspaper (the college newspaper), they immediately released several editions of the newspaper that highlighted my viral video that posted on September 17, 2020. My video and the news were spreading fast and compelled the college to act. To view all of the stories, simply do a Google search of the "Pioneer Newspaper" and read some of these stories and more:

> "OCCC Supports Discrimination, Harassment, and Civil Rights Violations: Professor Says"; "Professor, Community Reacts After Video Drops About Alleged Unethical OCCC Culture"; "Changes to Come: OCCC President Set to Retire In '21"; "Employees Claim College Doesn't Protect From Bad Bosses"; "Wounded Faculty Pass 2020 Resolution, Want to Say In New Administrative Hires"; "Controversial Admin, Gardner Withdraws From Leadership Roles"; "Professor Wants Hurtful OCCC Supervisors Cut Loose"; "College Administrators Offer Apologies For Employee Harm"; and several more stories that also highlighted what many believed to be gross misspending by the college President, i.e. spending more than $800K on office renovations, new furniture, etc.

2). On September 21, the OCCC Board of Regents accepted the President's retirement letter. The President said he would be "retiring" on July 2, 2021.

3). On September 23, 2020, I first reached out to the Oklahoma Education Association (OEA) and spoke to one of their legal advocates. OEA is an organization known for fighting battles for its roughly 40,000 members in public education.

I emailed them my initial video, newspaper articles, etc. regarding the punitive and retaliatory culture at the college. On October 14, 2020, the advocate discussed things with their team and believed there was enough to schedule a meeting with their legal team to discuss "specific goals and plans."

4). On October 2, 2020, the college set up "listening sessions" at the college that would serve as a forum for faculty, staff, and employees to provide our questions and voice concerns regarding the punitive and retaliatory culture. There were a series of 5 sessions that can be viewed on YouTube by searching "OCCC: Executive Team Listening Sessions." You will see starting in session #2 where I specifically call out one of the main administrators who myself and others believed to perpetuate the punitive and retaliatory culture. The new Chief of Staff acknowledged the culture at the college and vowed that she would do everything in her power to make significant changes. And she absolutely did!

The Chief of Staff was an outsider, so to speak, and not part of the history of the punitive and retaliatory culture, as she had only been at the college a short time.

So grateful for her, because she did not have to implement change. But I challenged her and the other Executive Team Member as well. And I left that Listening Session telling them both that "talk is cheap, and I want to see action. And I will continue my push for change."

5). On October 5th, 2020, I contacted the Higher Learning Commission (HLC) who provides the accreditation for the college, and filed a formal complaint in regards to a violation of "Criterion 2A: The institution establishes and follows policies and processes to ensure fair and ethical behavior on the part of its governing board, administration, faculty, and staff." I sent them several Pioneer Newspaper stories, my initial video and other videos, photos of the negative comments from others who had been victims, etc. And on October 23, 2020, after reviewing my complaint and evidence, the HLC determined that my complaint, "raises potential concerns…and due to these potential concerns…will conduct a further review of the institution."

6). Several other former and current faculty members had now felt comfortable coming out to speak against the college and to share their similar stories of harassment, targeting, discrimination, etc. which compelled the college to implement even more change in a timely manner.

7). It was announced on October 21, 2020, that one of the administrators I called out in the #2 Listening Session was no longer a part of the Executive Team and had "decided" to step down into a different role.

8). On October 23rd, KWTV Channel 9 airs a story, "Administrative Shake-Ups Continue at OCCC" that provided a summary of my initial video that started the movement for change and that certain administrators had stepped down from their powerful positions due to the culture that had been uncovered.

9). During the Listening Sessions, I continued to call out the other administrators that myself and others believed were perpetuating the toxic culture at the college.

10). The college announced on December 20, 2020, that the President's "retirement" was now effective January 1, 2021. This was 6 months earlier than the President had previously announced. Hmm…

11). The HR department had finally been separated from the control of administration and was now mutually exclusive and could finally be the final decision-makers in regards to grievances for faculty, staff, and employees.

12). More than 20 college policies were either removed, revised, or updated, as the new Chief of Staff (and now Executive Vice President) was on a mission to assist me and others in cleaning out the college, so to speak, and that meant first dealing with the HR department and college policies.

13). It was announced on Feb. 24, 2021, that the college had hired a new Vice President of Academic Affairs (VPAA). The majority of the college was extremely pleased with the decision, but we were all excited and happy that the supervisor, who had been serving in the interim position of VPAA would no longer be in that position. Hallelujah! Hallelujah! Hallelujah!

14). On March 3, 2021, it was announced that another administrator, one who many believed was a Central part of perpetuating the punitive and retaliatory culture at the college, would be retiring on June 30, 2021. According to many current and former faculty, staff, and employees, this administrator hurt a lot of people over the years and we were extremely glad to see they would be gone. When it was announced, there was a sigh of relief throughout the college because many believed this supervisor would remain in their position. When the announcement was sent via college email, I instantly received about 50 text messages, phone calls, and emails with a lot of individuals literally in tears thanking me for what I had done to affect change. It was a good day for the faculty, staff, and employees. And it was also a good day for the college.

15). On March 23, 2021, the OCCC Faculty Association passed a resolution in support of the recent changes in policies and leadership made by the Executive Vice President, who was the former Chief of Staff.

PHOTOS

Photo #1: Tattoos:

Photo #2: Tattoos:

Photo #3: Dad and Mom in their early 20s when they met:

Photo #4: Japanese grandparents (Shintaro and Chiyono Kimura):

Photo #5: Me and my grandfather:

Photo #6: Mom alone in Seminole feeling helpless:

Photo #7: Mom and dad when we lived with my cousins:

Photo #8: Me with long hair as a child:

Photo #9: My 80s hair:

Photo #10: Nikki around 1 year-old:

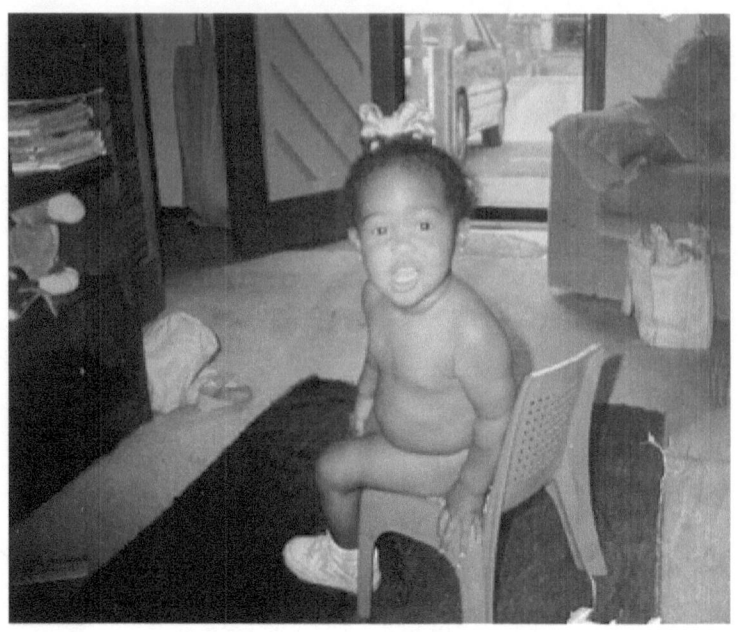

Photo #11: Me and Nikki bonding when she was a baby:

Photo #12: Me on the cover of a martial arts magazine:

Photo #13: 2014 family photo:

Photo #14: Me and mom at Ph.D. graduation. She was so proud:

Photo #15: My Ph.D. degree:

Photo #16: Text message I still have saved from Fred:

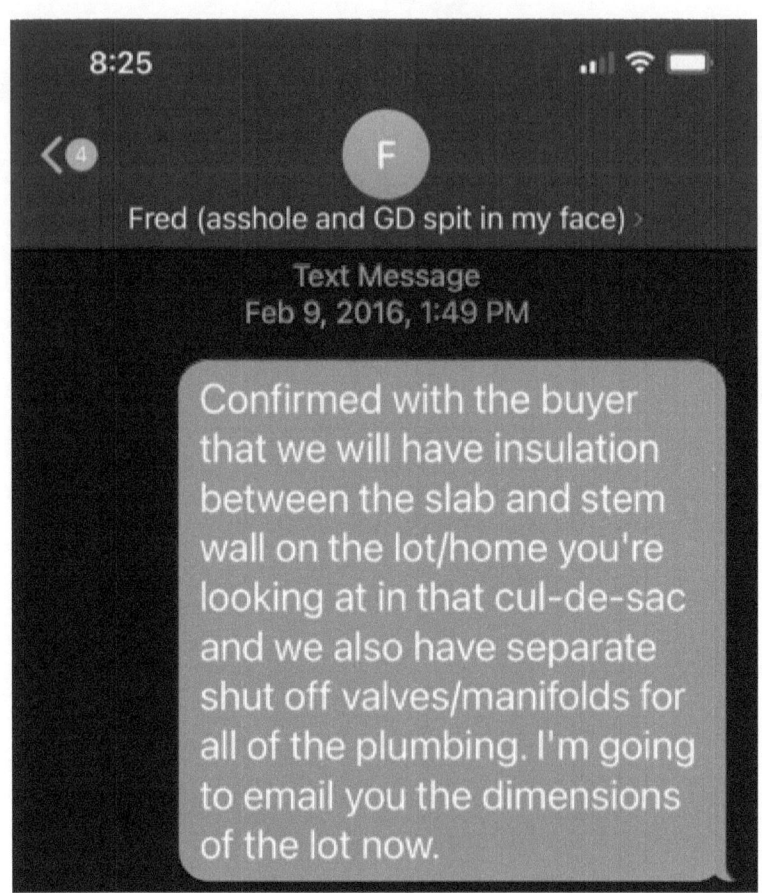

JOURNEY THROUGH THE HOODS · 225

Photo #17: First million-dollar sale check:

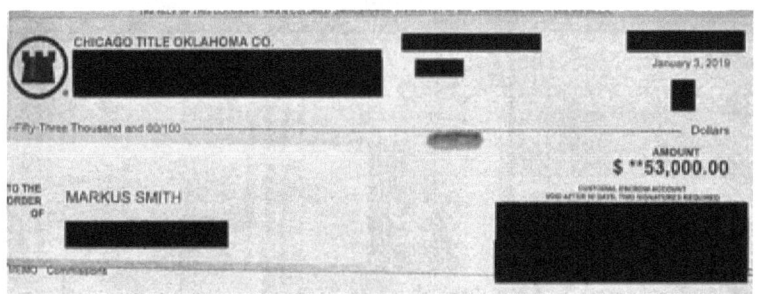

Photo #18: Messages from current and former OCCC faculty, staff, and employees:

> Dr-Markus Smith I am thank you. Good luck moving forward and I truly hope this brings about a positive change at OCCC.

> Dr-Markus Smith Thank you and thank you for bringing attention to this. I chose to leave my position at the College and go finish my degree largely because of these same issues.

> I wish I was better informed of my rights etc... while I was there. I was in such shock over everything happening, I didn't understand anything. The emotional toil that place took on me was unbelievable. I can't even drive to that campus without having a panic attack.

> I was physically backed up against a wall by two employees and HR did not believe me. I asked a question about a procedure I didn't understand and was written up for insubordination (simply for asking a question). When I

> Dr-Markus Smith I understand completely. Several of my friends who still work at the College have also expressed to me how much they appreciate what your doing as well. Know that you have a lot of people behind you!

> That's great. It's going to take a lot to undo the damage that's been done, but if anyone can do it, it is you. You are helping a lot of people heal.

> Thank you, Markus, for pursuing this. I taught at OCCC for many years and encountered various situations that didn't sit well. As a department chair, it was a tricky balance as I empathized with the adjunct faculty who usually got short shrifted. I had been an adjunct, so I understood their striving to become a full timer in the profession. There were others who encountered walls, both faculty and staff, and unfair practices, especially in HR. At some point, I learned that HR is not there to help employees. Duh. HR's role was to protect the institution and those at the top. It seems to work that way in most institutions and many corporations.

Photo #19: Messages from current and former OCCC faculty, staff, and employees (cont.):

> ▬▬▬▬▬ Just wanted to thank you for what you are doing. I wish I was in a situation where I could join you on this journey. But

> but while I do not know the ins and outs of your situation and experience, I know what I went through for 3 years almost derailed my career completely, but more importantly provided me with a clinical diagnosis of PTSD, anxiety, and depression. I kept documentation of everything from being

> Thank you again, Markus, for doing this! I'm sorry for everything you and others went through but it's been relieving in a way to know I wasn't the only one.

> Yes!! Finally this is getting out there! I am so proud of you standing up for those of us who were never allowed to and who are still facing this. Prayers for continued health and strength in this fight. 💕

> Yes! That is so great to hear. She has harmed so many people. It's like literally for the sake of humanity and education, she must be removed from having control over others' careers.

> Thank you so much. What you are doing is so crucial and brave. Hats 🎩 off to you.

> Hey Markus, I was one of the people who spoke to ▬▬▬ the investigative reporter, about leaving OCCC because I was being harrassed. So glad people are speaking out.

> I was so sorry to hear you went through so much there and I'm so glad you're speaking up. 🤍

> Thanks for your courage Dr. Smith, may God blessed you and protect you!!! Thanks for raising your voice and express what hurt us!!!

Photo #20: Comparing Nikki and the Asian genes from her "Nana". I'm often told I look my dad and Nikki looks like my mom:

Photo #21: Greyson-Markus as a baby with my mom in 2016:

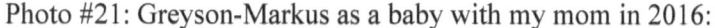

Photo #22: Greyson-Markus at 2 and 3 years-old:

Photo #23: Pedro (Chiweenie) and McGee (Labrador mix):

ABOUT THE AUTHOR

Dr. Smith currently resides in Oklahoma City, Oklahoma where he continues to teach as a professor of political science for nearly 20 years, as well as managing the Markus Smith Real Estate Team at Keller Williams Elite. He continues to be a philanthropist and serving his local communities. When he is not teaching or immersed in real estate, he enjoys spending time with family and friends, reading, and training in martial arts and boxing.

www.ingramcontent.com/pod-product-compliance
Lightning Source LLC
Chambersburg PA
CBHW030904080526
44589CB00010B/141